a celebration of contemporary
brazilian culture

brazil

Alcino Leite Neto

Samantha Pearson

introductions

Alcino Leite Neto

1.
The National Congress
of Brazil, Brasília,
Oscar Niemeyer, 1958

2.
São Paulo, 2010

3.
Dona Marta favela, Rio
de Janeiro, 2012

'Brazil is still a province. May God keep it that way for a long time!' wrote Manuel Bandeira, one of Brazil's most important poets, in 1932. There is no lack of irony in Bandeira's statement. Written at a time when the country was just beginning to forge a national identity, this former Portuguese province would contend with its provincial make-up and mindset for the best part of a century. Enormous in terms of both territory and in diversity of population and habitat, it would be unthinkable that this 'sleeping giant' should remain asleep for so long. Yet, perhaps because of its colonial past, or the geographical distance that separates it from the traditional economic and political centres of the world, and maybe even because of its vast size, for many years Brazil would remain relatively peripheral to international decision-making processes.

However, though historically scarred by weak economic and cultural ties with its Spanish-colonized neighbours, and entrenched within a political landscape where capitalism and democracy were painfully slow in maturing, Brazil harboured justifiable dreams of grandeur—dreams nourished throughout history by the country's leaders and intellectuals, as if Brazil was always destined to fulfil a unique, relevant role in global affairs; and in the eighty years since Bandeira wrote his poem, a number of factors—both economic and political—seem to have awoken the 'giant' and torn her away from provincialism.

All national identities are a construction, and Brazil's was built out of conflicts: white colonization and African slavery, highly disproportionate levels of income concentration and poverty, violence and cordiality, religiosity and sensuality... yet it is precisely because of the many conflicting aspects of Brazil's personality that it has so much to offer the worlds of culture and art.

Faced with this 'new' contender on the global stage, it is no surprise that people have started to become more curious about Brazil and to ask what Brazilians are capable of: as a guide to understanding contemporary Brazil, through two of its essential forces—culture and art—this book aims to answer that question. The focus is on contemporary production across the cultural spectrum—architecture, art, design, fashion, film, food, graphic design, music, photography and street art; but to truly understand what is happening today, one must understand what has happened in the past.

It was from 1922 onwards that the Modernist movement, in a gesture that was simultaneously an affirmation of national identity and an attempt to identify with foreign vanguards, initiated the rupture with the 'hitherto dominant Eurocentric academicism' and paved the way for the development of 'home-grown modern aesthetics' as Kiki Mazzucchelli explains in her introduction to the art chapter. From that moment on, art became one of the most proficient chroniclers of national reality and, at the same time, a powerful agent for the internationalization of Brazilian culture—the most evident manifestations of which were *bossa nova* and *Cinema Novo*, which bloomed during the 1950s and 1960s.

The Modernist period produced important interpreters of Brazilian history and exponents of the singularity of its civilization. Among them were the historian Sérgio Buarque de Holanda, and the sociologist Gilberto Freyre (with his controversial thesis on tropicology, referenced here by Marcelo Rezende in the street art chapter). It was not only intellectuals, however, who consolidated modern thought about Brazil. Some of the country's most

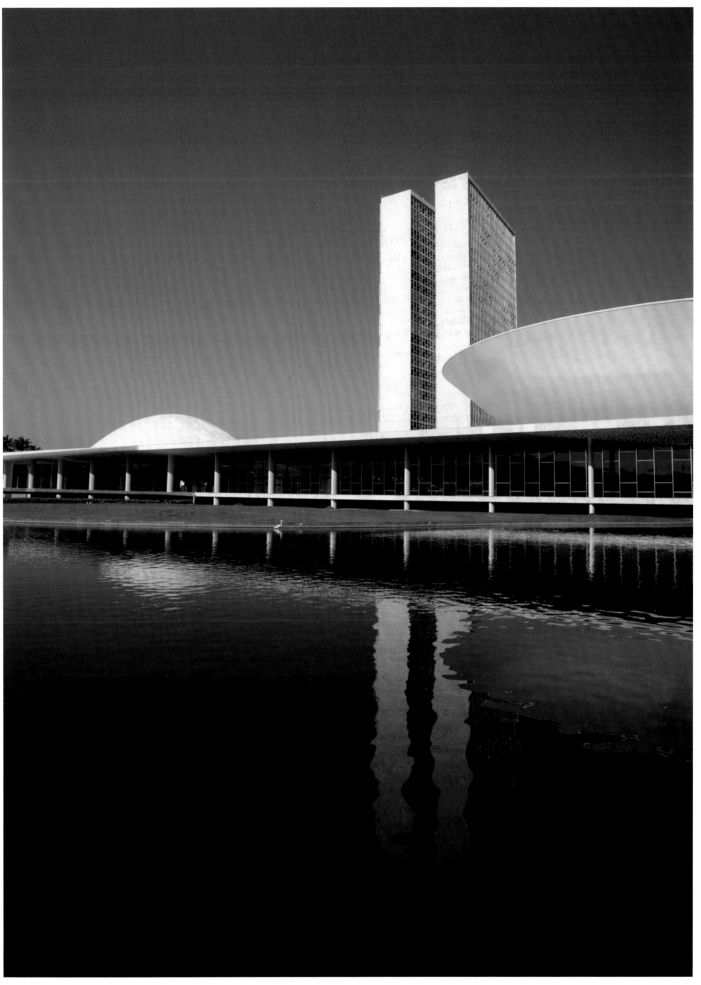

1.

2.

important twentieth century artists—from Oswald de Andrade to Hélio Oiticica, and Mário de Andrade to Glauber Rocha—became, themselves, active and crucial 'interpreters' of the country, some of them firmly engaged in a radical transformation of social and political life.

But the country, along with its problems and challenges, still interests many artists, even more so as Brazil's historical conflicts are still to be resolved. And, to face the 'Brazilian question' still implies, in a way, 'the constant interpellation of the potential left unexplored by the Modern process', an idea explored by Ana Vaz Milheiro, in her introduction to Brazilian architecture.

Without having quite concluded its modernization, Brazil arrived at the era of global technological capitalism with an economic vigour and social vitality that surprised even the most optimistic Brazilians. Behind the scenes, however, the country still nurses a series of old maladies, from violent social inequality (among the greatest in the world) to countless structural problems (ranging from education to the highway system). Brazil's present is fraught with paradoxes: the country encounters difficulties transporting its voluminous and precious agricultural output from its fields to its harbours, yet it has the most advanced Internet legislation in the world, passed in 2014.

It may no longer be a province, but Brazil remains a 'work in progress'. It is this heavy burden—that of a country still being built and a people still being formed—that causes such anxiety amongst Brazilians and such surprise amongst foreigners: here, in Brazil, the future has just begun.

3.

Samantha Pearson

4.
Copacabana beach
promenade, designed by
Burle Marx in 1969-72,
Rio de Janeiro

It was both a fitting and delightfully bizarre tribute to Brazil's greatest modern architect. Only a few weeks after Oscar Niemeyer's death in December 2012, graffiti artist Eduardo Kobra took it upon himself to cover the side of one of São Paulo's skyscrapers with a psychedelic painting of the architect's face. 'His works were so important he deserved a space like this', explains Kobra, who grew up in the city's poor outskirts and spent most of his teenage years in and out of police custody. After persuading the office building's tenants to pay for the paint and getting a local restaurant and hotel to provide free food and accommodation, he and three friends set to work. For the next 40 days, they braved Brazil's tropical heat and downpours to depict every last wrinkle of the 104-year-old's face, producing what is now considered one of the world's most remarkable examples of street art.

Niemeyer, a staunch communist celebrated for his sinuously curved buildings, may have been somewhat baffled by his final resting place — a mundanely linear office block wedged between two banks. But Kobra's Olympic swimming pool-sized mural is nonetheless the perfect celebration of the architect's lifelong battle to democratize urban space as well as proof of the bold new creative spirit of the modern Brazil he helped create.

Only a generation ago, the Latin American country was no more than an exotic outpost on the global arts circuit. Censorship under Brazil's military dictatorship from 1964 to 1985 stifled artistic expression, while hyperinflation in the 1980s and 1990s crushed the country's creative industries. However, after a decade of political and economic stability, Brazil's cultural scene is more vibrant than ever, placing it at the forefront of the creative world. Brazilian painters are among the most coveted by museums and auction houses, Rio de Janeiro's fashion designers are dressing the rich and famous, and even the most obscure Amazonian fruits have become culinary staples thanks to Brazil's pioneering chefs.

The country's recent growth has also brought diversity. As the world's seventh-biggest economy, Brazil has attracted a fresh wave of immigrants from nations such as Bolivia, Angola and Haiti, adding new stitches to Brazil's already rich racial tapestry. Perhaps most important of all, though, has been the rise of families, such as Kobra's, out of poverty and into both the country's middle class and the national consciousness. Between 2003 and 2014 around 60 million people — equivalent to the entire UK population — entered Brazil's middle class, revealing a vast underbelly of raw untapped talent that the powers that be are still learning how to accommodate. It will be a long process. Os Gêmeos, twin brothers from São Paulo whose street art is so popular abroad that Louis Vuitton commissioned them to design a silk scarf in 2012, are sometimes still treated as vandals by the city's government.

However, many of Brazil's greatest achievements over the past decade are now difficult to reverse. While the country still struggles with its age-old problems of corruption and inefficiency, its new middle class is here to stay. From the catwalks of Rio to the kitchens of Belém, this book takes the reader on a journey across this vast new Brazil, showcasing the top talent across disciplines from art to music and pointing out the exciting new names off the beaten track. Each chapter attempts to address the question: in a continental country fifteen times the size of France, what defines Brazil's creative spirit?

4.

In São Paulo, the city's most innovative creators have actually risen in protest against their surroundings. Faced with the oppressive greyness of the concrete megalopolis, artists have gone to extraordinary lengths to bring colour and humanity back to the lives of its 11 million residents. Alongside audacious graffiti, activist craft groups have taken to knitting patterned sleeves for the trunks of the city's few remaining trees. But while São Paulo may not have the looks, it certainly has the cash. Already Latin America's business capital, São Paulo now moonlights as the hub of Brazil's booming commercial art market, whose revenues are rising at close to thirty per cent per year. Most of this growth is coming from dynamic new collectors—in 2013 a third of all galleries in Brazil were under three years old. Home to the São Paulo Biennial (Sp-Arte), the world's second-oldest (and Latin America's biggest) commercial art fair, the city has also played a pivotal role in selling Brazilian art to the world and in bringing the world to Brazil.

A six-hour drive northeast, Rio de Janeiro's forested mountains and spectacular white sands are a source of bitter envy in São Paulo. The effortless transcendental beauty of Brazil's former capital has turned Rio into a mecca for creative talent, a tropical Paris. From Tunga to Cildo Meireles, the country's most influential artists were either born or moved here—many even hang out together on the same stretch of beach. Among collectors' favourites is Beatriz Milhazes, known as Brazil's 'Kandinsky' for her carnivalesque geometric paintings—she became an overnight sensation in 2008 when *O Mágico* (The Magician) sold at Sotheby's in New York for just over a million dollars (half a million pounds). Meanwhile, the popular Rio Fashion Show competes with São Paulo Fashion Week for the attention of the world's fashionistas. Even the city's drug-ridden slums have provided creative inspiration, launching the career of the cinema director Fernando Meirelles, whose blockbuster film *City of God* was nominated for an Oscar in 2004.

Just over 600 km (372 miles) inland, the state of Minas Gerais is famous for rather more mundane things: its mines and its cheese. But buried among its verdant hills is one of the world's most remarkable outdoor art parks, Inhotim—a type of Disneyland for art-lovers where names such as Matthew Barney sit alongside Brazil's top talent. The 3,000-acre complex created by mining tycoon Bernardo Paz is testament to the influence of private collectors in Brazil, who largely call the shots as underfunded public galleries struggle to keep up. With the growth of the last decade, these billionaires have been joined by a generation of more humble aficionados—lawyers and university professors who pay for works in multiple instalments, opening up a vast market for younger (and cheaper) artists.

After a gruelling ten-hour drive into Brazil's central scrubland, Niemeyer's white spaceship-like buildings begin to emerge from the red dust. Here in Brazil's capital city Brasília, where Niemeyer designed everything from taxi ranks to the presidential palace, it is easy to understand why younger architects have struggled to move forwards. Marcelo Ferraz and Francisco Fanucci of the firm Brasil Arquitetura are among those who have managed it. In 2012 their firm completed Praças das Artes, a prize-winning music and dance centre in São Paulo, proving that there could be life after Niemeyer. (In a bizarre twist of fate, Niemeyer died only a few hours after it was opened.) In the early 1980s, the duo also assisted Lina Bo Bardi on the conversion of an abandoned factory into the popular SESC Pompeia arts centre—a format that would be replicated by London's Tate Modern almost two decades later.

After three hours in a plane heading further north, the dust-filled air is replaced with the heavy humidity of the Amazon jungle. It is here that one of the country's most celebrated photographers, Sebastião Salgado, lived among Yanomami Indians for his 2013 publication, *Genesis*—a study of the world's untouched communities. However, Brazil's forested northern region is not only home to endangered tribes, but some 17 million Brazilians, who would rather stalk friends on Facebook than wild animals. Mainly recent arrivals to the middle class, they are making their voices heard for the first time—and some are louder than others. Gaby Amarantos, known as the Beyoncé of the Amazon, has won over huge audiences with her brand of *Tecno Brega* ('Cheesy Techno'), a fusion of electronic pop and local dance styles such as *Carimbó*, itself an African-Portuguese invention.

Since the *Tropicalismo* movement of the 1960s, which championed the appropriation of disparate influences to create something unique, Brazil has continuously 'cannibalized' other cultures. However, over the past decade Brazil has learnt the art of cannibalism in its truest sense—the rediscovery and digestion of its own hidden talent, the stars who have been ignored for years but who offer endless possibilities for the future.

No one understands this better perhaps than Alex Atala, Brazil's top chef, who spends his life making journeys across the country, picking through infinite combinations of ingredients to delight the world's palates. During an interview for a Brazilian foreign ministry publication, Atala was asked to explain Brazil's obsession with buffet restaurants—one of the few places in the world where it is socially acceptable to pile sushi, chips, lasagne, and a steak on to the same plate. 'I think it reflects what Brazil really is', he replied. 'A patchwork of cultures that are respected and unified in a singular and positive way.'

5.

Marcio Kogan / StudioMK27

Paulo Mendes da Rocha

João Filgueiras Lima

MMBB

GrupoSP

Carla Juaçaba

Isay Weinfeld

Brasil Arquitetura

UNA Arquitetos

Ana Vaz Milheiro

architecture

It could be argued that the history of contemporary Brazilian architecture began as a written narrative, with Gregori Warchavchik's 1925 manifesto, *Acerca da Architectura Moderna*, before it even became a constructed form. 'Our architecture must be solely rational, it must base itself only on logic, and this logic must be opposed to those who are forcefully attempting to imitate some style,' Warchavchik claimed. The movement gained international visibility at the New York World's Fair in 1939 through the Brazilian pavilion designed by Lucio Costa and Oscar Niemeyer, with landscaping by Burle Marx. Costa decoded the pavilion's poetic, abstract language for the officials: 'the undulating rhythm of the land which the greater body of construction accentuates is repeated in the marquee, the ramp, the retaining walls of the ground floor, the mezzanine, the auditorium, etc., concurring to lend the whole an original, unmistakable and extremely pleasant feature.'

From 1943 onwards, international circles began to take interest in what was happening in Brazil, intrigued by its avidly Modern architecture. *Brazil Builds*, an exhibition at the New York Museum of Modern Art that year, confirmed the influence of Le Corbusier, who had visited the country in 1929 and later in 1936 and who consulted on buildings such as the Ministry of Education and Health, which was under construction in Rio de Janeiro at the time. The MoMA exhibition demonstrated works by Rino Levi, Marcelo Roberto, Lucio Costa and Burle Marx, plus the pioneering work of Warchavchik. However, the expansion of this Modern aesthetic was slow at first, due mainly to the immensity of the territory: projects were concentrated in Rio de Janeiro and São Paulo, with lesser examples in Recife, Olinda, Niterói, Salvador and Fortaleza. In Belo Horizonte, the capital of the state of Minas Gerais, Niemeyer's chapel of Saint Francis of Assisi was yet to be completed. Here, the architect experimented with a new organic form, made possible with the use of reinforced concrete. It was the result of an architecture that consciously rejected 'repeated, cold and geometric solutions' as Niemeyer explained, distancing itself from European lessons — namely, Le Corbusier's initial purism. Later, Affonso Eduardo Reidy would confirm the distinctive feature of Brazilian architecture and its visceral propensity to plasticity. 'Certainly, the simple fact of a construction attending to purely functional ends is not a sufficient condition for it to deserve the designation of a work of architecture.'

Walter Gropius visited Reidy's Conjunto Residencial Pedregulho, built in the industrial neighbourhood of São Cristóvão in Rio de Janeiro in 1946 to promote the proximity of residence and workplace, announcing it as a 'model as much from the aesthetic point-of-view as the social, not only for Brazil but for the entire world'. Pedregulho's completion would demonstrate the confidence of Brazilian architecture to follow its own model, no longer restricted by its colonial inheritance, and positioning itself internationally as an emerging, emancipated culture.

It was the construction of the new capital Brasília in the 1950s that proved the Brazilian aptitude for monumental scale, which Modern architecture promoted as necessary after World War II. Brasília was the electoral promise of newly elected president Juscelino Kubitschek (former mayor of Belo Horizonte and governor of the state of Minas Gerais) who had been behind the commissioning of Niemeyer's Pampulha projects, and saw the national capital move from Rio to a more central geographical location. The new city was designed to house 500,000 inhabitants. Today, it is home to more than 2.5 million individuals. Twenty-six proposals from teams led by Brazilian architects were presented for the design of the city and the result was announced in March 1957, not without some controversy. In the final report on Lucio Costa's winning project, the jury

1.

1.
The National Congress
of Brazil, Brasília,
Oscar Niemeyer, 1958

2.
Itamaraty Palace,
Brasília, Oscar
Niemeyer, 1960

3.
Church of Saint
Francis, Pampulha,
Belo Horizonte, Oscar
Niemeyer, 1940

2.

3.

declared, 'It is new; it is free and open; it is disciplined without being rigid'. The designs most clearly affiliated with the Congrès Internationaux d'Architecture Moderne (CIAM) ended up being rejected in favour of what Eric Mumford later described as the competition proposal that most resembled 'a traditional capital'. Great expectations were placed on the construction of this new city; however, less than ten years after the plans were unveiled, as Brazil came to terms with a military dictatorship, Costa reflected that 'the simple change of the capital could not resolve the fundamental contradictions' of the country. The issues that critics raised about the new capital were generally structural: the city 'denied', as Atsushi Ueda testified, 'the existence of people. Nothing was provided for the pedestrian'.

After 1968, the year that signalled the tightening of restrictions on individual liberties, what Brazilian architecture lost in its relationship with the zeitgeist, it gained in formal exoticism. The hedonism of Oscar Niemeyer, who by then had emigrated to Europe, made him a progressively spectral figure: 'I produce the architecture that gives me pleasure, naturally connected to my roots and to my country,' he said in 1973. A new chapter had begun. The desire to act on a supranational scale had diminished, which weakened the export capacity of Brazilian architecture as a concept, but also opened the way for regional expression. São Paulo-born Joaquim Guedes pointed out the new trend. 'The solutions in the accepted taste were light, opportunistic, and in the end, ignored Brazil because of a methodological incompatibility.'

In São Paulo, a lack of publicly-funded projects of social and architectural interest manifested itself in a swathe of privately-funded single-family houses designed by Guedes and his contemporaries in the Jardin neighbourhood of the city. In an involuntary ideological subversion of the more doctrinaire Modernism, the bourgeois house was maintained as a privileged space for experimentation.

Elsewhere in the city, other architects such as Ruy Ohtake, Carlos Millan, João Walter Toscano and Paulo Mendes da Rocha concentrated on the foundation of an architectural culture with modern roots and a sense of social responsibility. This production had its defining moment with the construction of the Faculdade de Arquitetura e Urbanismo at the University of São Paulo (FAU-USP) designed by João Vilanova Artigas and Carlos Cascaldi (1961–68) and hailed as the greatest expression of *brutalismo paulista*. In the second half of the 1960s the rhetoric was radicalized, demanding an alternative to capitalist production. The *Arquitetura Nova* (New Architecture) movement, an adaptation of the *estética da fome* (the aesthetics of famine) by Sérgio Ferro, Flávio Império and Rodrigo Lefèvre, sought to revolutionize the construction site: design, worker and social programme were entrenched, creating a perceptible lineage in the contemporary production of the city. In other parts of the country, regional architectural styles were more informed by climate and environment: the brise-soleil (first popularized by Le Corbusier in his 1930s Algerian projects) and the *cobogó*—a type of perforated brick invented in Pernambuco, used as a decorative element and as a way of providing natural ventilation and light, both enjoyed increasing popularity. Meanwhile, the responsibility of maintaining international expectations of Brazilian architecture fell to Lina Bo Bardi.

The political and architectural landscape changed with the return to democracy in 1985, and it was at the end of this decade that Paulo Mendes da Rocha was more regularly publicized (anticipating the Pritzker Architecture Prize, which he went on to receive in 2006). His works from the 1950s, alongside contemporary buildings, began to be dissected by international critics. The Museu Brasileiro de Escultura (Brazilian Sculpture Museum) in São Paulo, which he designed at the end of the 1980s, secured his role as a leading figure in Brazilian architecture, serving as a counterpoint to a Postmodernism that, on an international level, already found itself exhausted. In a continual process of purification, his works attained a minimalist appearance, a fundamental aspect of his rediscovery. It was confirmation that, in Brazil, Modern architecture was still very much alive.

The work of Mendes da Rocha, and of some of his São Paulo colleagues, also symbolized the Brazilian resistance to approaching Modern architecture as an historical period, making it difficult to position contemporary practice within the Postmodern chronology to which it effectively belonged. At the turn of the millennium, these aspects began to be questioned again and the debate was re-opened, highlighting the lack of recognized quality Postmodern architecture, and the absence of critical questioning of Modern works. The principal argument focused on the failure of social design, and on the delay in applying progressive social dynamics. Not even the Conjunto Residencial Pedregulho was spared: it was accused of negligence towards the habits of unprivileged communities, and of imposing imported models of dwellings. Brasília was highlighted as the worst failure—dismissed as a segregated place, with no social improvement. Descriptions of the violent repression to which the *candangos*—the workers from the northeast who had migrated to the country's central plain to construct the new capital—had been subjected, contaminated the readings about the city's architecture and urbanism.

Recent Brazilian architecture is not based on the creation of new facts, but on the constant interpellation of the potential left unexplored by the Modern process. It does not embark on a sort of neo-historicism, in the sense that the history of the country's architecture is seen as under construction. Indeed, the difficult rehabilitation of old buildings from the period between 1925–1970, which were allowed to fall into disrepair, demonstrates that there is no collective notion of their status as historic monuments. Yet, despite inadequate protection of these historic sites, architects are, in general, well aware of the significance of this period within international history and understand the importance of upholding the legacy left by Modernism. Frequent references to the Modern as national identity tend to curb the progression of more speculative practices: the best Brazilian architecture is that which positions itself as the exception and not the rule, standing in opposition to the dominant technocracy in city-making.

Interest in prefabrication systems and the industrialization of Brazilian construction remains a central theme. During the 1980s, in Abadiânia (Goiás), João Filgueiras Lima installed an artisanal factory for prefabricated building elements applied to the production of small-scale equipment. The SARAH Network of Rehabilitation Hospitals—a new model of public health-care active since 1976, benefited from this experimentation, with a number of new sites built across the country. Each new project, constructed from prefabricated systems in steel and reinforced concrete, was adapted for regional labour structures, in order to provide jobs for local labour forces. The Lago Norte site in Brasília, (1995–2003) is an example of how contemporary Brazilian architecture strives to achieve a Modern progressive utopia, combining function, technique and work force organization.

Large-scale initiatives, such as the Centros Educacionais Unificados (CEU) of São Paulo (Alexandre Delijaicov, André Takiya and Wanderley Ariza), a municipal project launched in 2001, have taken advantage of prefabrication as a cost and time efficient mode of construction. Offering educational, cultural and sports programmes, the forty-five different sites across the city have helped regenerate the area — typically the *favelas* (slums) — where they are located. These informally occupied areas with no real infrastructure have great scope for 'urbanization'. Abstraction, repetition and monumentality are the key features of the architecture of these units, making the CEU a new type of public building, based on the programme's social character.

Some of the most innovative projects in contemporary Brazilian architecture involve the transformation of previously abandoned sites, creating a dialogue between old and new — a trend that has been popular since the 1970s. Notable historical examples include Lina Bo Bardi's SESC Pompéia (São Paulo, 1977, with André Vainer and Marcelo Carvalho Ferraz) and Paulo Mendes da Rocha's project for the Pinacoteca do Estado (São Paulo, 1993) which reclaimed the previous Liceu de Artes e Ofícios, turning it into into a museological space and establishing itself as a model for these kinds of projects. Mendes da Rocha applied a more radical approach to the Centro Cultural SESI/FIESP (1996) project, which saw a huge steel structure attached to the facade of Rino Levi's existing brutalist headquarters of the Federação de Indústrias de São Paulo (1969–79). Moreover, in large Brazilian metropolises such as São Paulo, the maintenance of old, eclectic buildings or deactivated industrial structures often goes beyond the simple act of material conservation as a response to predatory urban practices. For example, rather than besieging an existing building, the transformation of USP's Centro Universitário Maria Antônia by Una Arquitetos (Cristiane Muniz, Fábio Valentim, Fernanda Barbara, Fernando Viégas, 2002) opened up a public space in the interior of the block, mimicking more traditional city buildings. Thus, a new square, born from the reconfiguration of two pre-existing buildings, strengthened the cohesion of the site.

But it is as part of a process of decentralization and of fostering cultural tourism that rehabilitation has emerged as a social phenomenon of greatest importance. In little-known municipalities, architectural projects have spurred new economic opportunities. In Ilópolis, in Rio Grande do Sul, the Museu do Pão (Bread Museum), by Brasil Arquitetura (Francisco de Paiva Fanucci and Marcelo Carvalho Ferraz), transforms a piece of vernacular architecture: the century-old rehabilitated mill building in conjunction with a new glass and concrete pavilion — a work of juxtaposition that recalls the artisanal compositions of Bo Bardi, with whom Carvalho Ferraz collaborated. Indeed, the Brasil Arquitetura offices have realized many such projects throughout the country for cultural programmes such as the Conjunto KKKK (Registro, São Paulo, 1996–2001) and the Museu Rodin in Salvador (2002–06), whose *modus operandi* has refined the vernacular-rooted brutalist expression that Bo Bardi symbolized. The Praça das Artes in São Paulo (2006–13), a cultural complex dedicated to music and dance, is perhaps the most successful example of this experiment, helping to regenerate the recently neglected historic city centre. The fragmented concrete building occupies vacant lots and weaves in and out of existing buildings, incorporating them in the design. The building's concrete is tinted with an ochre pigment, giving the whole structure an earthy quality.

Over this last decade, the commitment to hosting three international sporting events — the Pan-American Games in 2007, the 2014 World Cup and the Olympic Games in 2016 — has meant a proliferation of construction projects and the modernization of existing venues dating from the 1950s,

1960s and 1970s. For the World Cup, twelve Brazilian cities have witnessed new or converted stadiums: Manaus, Fortaleza, Natal, Recife, Salvador, Cuiabá, Brasília, Belo Horizonte, Rio de Janeiro, São Paulo, Curitiba and Porto Alegre. The projects were granted to a consortium of construction companies with local, international and multidisciplinary offices. Some involved the participation of architects from older generations and others involved specialized teams active in emerging countries, such as gmp, Architekten von Gerkan and Marg und Partners. These projects have also allowed younger teams to gain recognition.

Other positive results of these events can be seen in programmes such as Morar Carioca, launched in 2010 by Rio's Municipal Department of Housing, whose long-term goal is to improve the city's *favelas* by 2020. These interventions have worked towards increasing the self-esteem and safety of people living in notoriously violent neighbourhoods. The project for the Complexo de Manguinhos, by Jorge Mario Jáuregui and team (Metrópolis Projetos Urbanos, 2009–12), began with elevating the train that previously divided the *favela* and included a new linear park, a library, new residential blocks and a school. Cable cars made hillside accessibility simpler for the pedestrian.

However, it is in the domain of popular housing that architects have been called upon to present their vision for Brazilian cities, participating in local programmes such as Habita Sampa (2004) or, more recently, in the Renova SP (2011) national public bid for architecture and city planning projects, launched by São Paulo's Municipal Department of Housing (SEHAB). The latter covers twenty-two areas indentified as 'Perimeters of Integrated Action', and seeks to re-equip extensive peripheral regions of the city occupied by *favelas*. These operations contrast with the federal mega-programme *Minha Casa, Minha Vida* (My House, My Life), which supports the production of housing for families with gross monthly incomes of up to R$5,000 (£1,330) throughout Brazil. The suburban implantation of new neighbourhoods in regions with deficiencies in infrastructure, transportation or services, makes *Minha Casa, Minha Vida* a generic 'anti-city' and a potentially segregating programme. As an alternative, architects continue to propose models that promote social and urban cohesion in disadvantaged communities, responding to some of the criticism targeted at the lack of social objectivity of the original modern large projects.

In São Paulo, former *favela* areas, recently converted to expansion spaces and new business centres, have currently been transformed to the benefit of these populations, confirming their right to a dwelling. The housing development Jardim Edite (MMBB, Marta Moreira, Milton Braga and Fernando de Mello Franco, and H+F, Eduardo Ferroni and Pablo Hereñú, 2011), located next to one of the new financial sectors of the city, combines services and housing, maintaining inhabitants close to urban facilities and raising expectations of employability. It is a monumental development, built over a disassembled *favela*, which gathers 252 families in units of 50 m² (538 sq ft). Without the naiveté of the past, which sought to alter ways of life, the buildings make available a minimum set of community provisions (restaurant, basic health clinic and daycare). Here, architecture functions as a means of inclusion by imposing an elevated standard to the design and urban conception of the buildings.

The commitment that these housing projects must have to the city is equally crucial for the construction of a collective urbanity. The residential building on Rua Simpatia in São Paulo (GrupoSP, 2007–10) follows examples from the 1980s, developed by Mendes da Rocha in relation to dealing with difficult topography. The resourceful solution of dividing the block into parking and service areas below and housing wings above allows for the creation of open communal space at ground level, enabling circulation and interaction. It stands in contrast to the more rigid and closed private initiatives that occupy impermeable residential lots.

Brazil's future involves the resolution of some of the dilemmas that architects face in cities such as São Paulo, the fourth most populous metropolis in the world. The continued debate regarding urban development furthers the possibility of finding a model based on sustainable sources. This can be seen with the urban plan of Parque Dom Pedro II (Una arquitetos, H+F, Metrópole and Lume, 2010). Here, the architects promoted the reconstruction of the landscape's original low land condition, in opposition to the car-focused masterplan models the city has been subjected to since the 1950s. The work methodology, based on cooperation between autonomous firms, reveals a collective approach committed to the consolidation of a shared reflection. There is now an awareness that the high density of existent infrastructure ended up, paradoxically, becoming an obstacle to the mobility of populations. The demolition of viaducts and new emphasis on public transportation reflects the desire to 'start over', opening clearings in order to re-urbanize. It is an optimistic discourse that does not exclude a large-scale solution, still capable of proposing a global view of the metropolis, and integrating geography, demography and landscape. Despite the potentially demiurge gesture, the new plan implies a revision of the most orthodox, Modern, progressive sense and brings about a vision that is 'native' because it is rooted in the conditions of the country and of the region. It is inscribed into a history that continues on, now more focused and fearless than before.

4.
São Paulo Art Museum (MASP), São Paulo, Lina Bo Bardi, 1957–68

5.
Ministry of Education and Health, Rio de Janeiro, Lucio Costa and team, 1936–43

6.
Brazilian Museum of Sculpture, São Paulo, Paulo Mendes da Rocha, 1985–95

4.

5.

6.

Marcio Kogan / StudioMK27

Marcio Kogan was born — quite literally — in the shadow of his father: engineer Aron Kogan was responsible for erecting the 170m (558 ft) Altino Arantes building in São Paulo, which for decades was the tallest skyscraper in Brazil. Marcio propelled himself in another direction — after venturing briefly into the world of cinema (he directed a feature film in 1988) he decided that architecture was his vocation.

The straight lines, pure forms and clean details imprinted in his projects from restaurants, luxury hotels and museums to apartment buildings and private residences, act as an eternal tribute to the great masters of the Modernist movement such as Lina Bo Bardi, Vilanova Artigas, Oscar Niemeyer and Lucio Costa. 'I have always admired Brazilian Modernism' Kogan says. 'It's surprising to me that in the early and mid-twentieth century, Brazil produced the projects that it did... so simple and elegant. A lesson for our superfluous world in crisis.'

In the early 1980s, he opened StudioMK27, an architectural firm that practises a democratic, collaborative work ethic. Every architect involved in a project becomes co-author with Kogan, and the studio's staff is incredibly multidisciplinary: knowledge about art, music, cinema, economy and politics is just as important in their architecture as knowledge about design, visual programming and urbanism.

Since 2001, StudioMK27 has won more than 50 Brazilian prizes, with distinction for the Wallpaper Design Awards, D&AD 'Yellow Pencil' and LEAF Awards, and has become three-time finalist in the World Architecture Festival.

Born in São Paulo, 1954

1.

1.
Lee House, Porto Feliz,
2012

2.
Cube House, São Paulo,
2012

3.
Studio R, São Paulo,
2012

2.

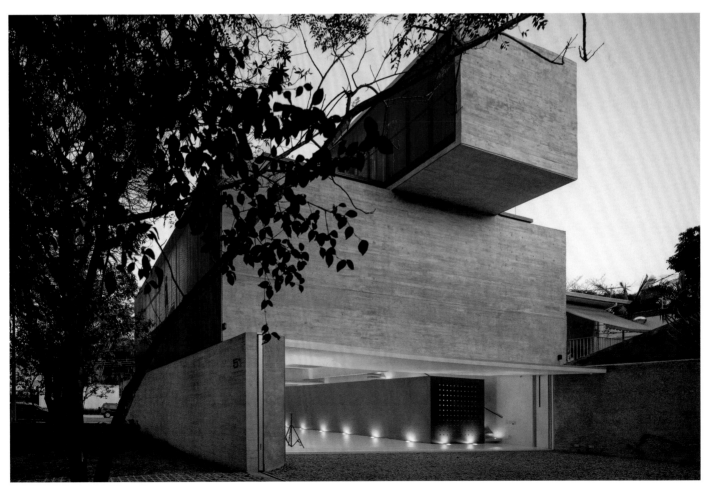

3.

4.

5.

4–5.
V4 House, São Paulo,
2011

6–8.
Studio SC, São Paulo,
2011

6.

7.

8.

Paulo Mendes da Rocha

In 2006, Paulo Mendes da Rocha became the second Brazilian to receive the greatest international architecture award — the Pritzker Architecture Prize — which Oscar Niemeyer was awarded in 1988. Mendes da Rocha attended the Mackenzie School of Architecture and Urbanism, graduating in 1954, before opening his office in 1955. Working almost exclusively in Brazil, Mendes da Rocha has been designing buildings since then, with his first early masterpiece, the Athletic Club of São Paulo, completed in 1957.

Many of Mendes da Rocha's projects are constructed from concrete, in a style some refer to as 'Brazilian Brutalism' and they are clearly influenced by the work of João Vilanova Artigas. When asked about the 'Brazilian' nature of his work, he responded, 'maybe it's best to say there isn't, nor should there be, any "Brazilian architecture". It doesn't make much sense to me, to defend a national character. What one may imagine, in a healthy way, is that there is something unique in the experience of América.'

During the military dictatorship, Mendes da Rocha was banned from practicing and teaching architecture, but after the fall of the regime in the 1980s, his work was rediscovered internationally and it gained new relevance. He has contributed many notable cultural buildings to São Paulo and is widely credited for enhancing and revitalizing the city. He has received many awards, including the Mies van der Rohe prize for Latin American Architecture (2000), which paid tribute to the architect's respectful renovation of the Pinacoteca do Estado, Sao Paulo's oldest fine arts museum.

Born in Vitória, 1928

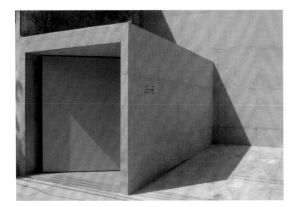

1.

2.

3.

1–3.
Leme Gallery, São Paulo, 2004

4.
Pinacoteca do Estado, São Paulo, 1998

5.
Leme Gallery, São Paulo, 2004

4.

5.

João Filgueiras Lima

Born in 1932, João Filgueiras Lima (known affectionately as Lelé) grew up in Rio de Janeiro. After going through military school, he attended the Escola das Belas Artes, and graduated in architecture from the Federal University of Rio de Janeiro in 1956. After his studies, he worked as a draftsman for the Retirement and Pension Institute (IAP) and in 1957, they commissioned him to develop and monitor the construction of the workers' lodgings in Brasília. He moved to Brazil's future capital at the beginning of its construction and conducted research on industrial components for large-scale building projects.

Lelé's work is notable for combining industrial methods — like series production of prefabricated components — with free, often sinuous forms assimilated from his close collaboration with Oscar Niemeyer.

In 1976, the SARAH Network of Rehabilitation Hospitals was formed, and the Musculoskeletal System unit allowed Lelé to explore new concepts in hospital design, together with the orthopaedist Aloysio Campos da Paz. He set up 'hospital factories' to produce not only building components, but also medical appliances for the network of hospitals. The most significant technical achievement in this area was the high-standard systems of ventilation and natural lighting, which played a part in the recovery process of in-patients. The buildings he designed for the SARAH network would come to define his career and style.

Born in Rio de Janeiro, 1932 (died 2014)

1.

2.

1.
Children's
Rehabilitation Centre,
Rio de Janeiro, 2001

2–4.
The International
Centre for Neuroscience,
Brasília, 2002

3.

4.

MMBB

MMBB Architects was founded in 1991 by three architects, Fernando de Mello Franco, Marta Moreira and Milton Braga, all graduates from FAU-USP between 1986 and 1987. Their designs are often the product of associations and partnerships with other architects and engineering consultancy companies, and they have a particularly close relationship with the architect Paulo Mendes da Rocha. These collaborations have offered the firm the opportunity to develop large-scale projects both within Brazil and abroad, such as the Museu dos Coches (2009–2014), in Lisbon. The association with engineering consultancy companies has led to the development of a number of infrastructural designs, such as bus station terminuses and tunnels, underground car parks, highway toll booths and pedestrian walkways.

They have also designed a series of private residences and housing projects. The Jardim Edite Social Housing Complex was commissioned to replace a *favela* located in one of the most significant areas of recent growth in the financial sector of São Paulo.

The MMBB architects also extend their activities to the cultural and academic sphere, organizing a series of cultural events, exhibitions and biennials as well as developing an academic programme of teaching and research. In 2013, founding member Fernando de Mello Franco was elected the Secretary of Urban Development in São Paulo.

Founded in São Paulo, 1991

1.

2.

1–2.
Ribeirão Preto House
(with Angelo Bucci),
Ribeirão Preto, 2001

3.
Dental Clinic
(with Angelo Bucci),
Orlândia, 2000

4.
Romana House and
Studio, São Paulo, 2006

3.

4.

5.

6.

7.

5–7.
Rolim de Camargo
residence, São Paulo,
2008

8–10.
Jardim Edite Social
Housing Complex, São
Paulo, 2013

8.

9.

10.

GrupoSP

Founded in 2004, GrupoSP is a collective based in São Paulo that currently consists of Alvaro Puntoni (1965), João Sodré (1978), João Yamamoto (1979) and André Nunes (1986), all former students at the University of São Paulo's School of Architecture and Urbanism (FAU-USP). GrupoSP is not a traditional architectural office, but rather a flexible organization that supports collaborations and partnerships with other architects and professionals interested in the discussion around living spaces and urban planning.

In recent years they have dedicated themselves to architectural competitions and projects for NGOs and public institutions, working on a number of educational buildings. In 2006, they designed the Ataliba Leonel School on the periphery of São Paulo, in a working-class neighbourhood where scarce public facilities become the focus of local social life. Columns rise the full height of the volume, while the subdivisions of window frames

and screens provide a smaller, more human scale. Timber mesh screens protect the corridors leading to the classrooms and shield the views into, and out of, the study spaces. Both visually and physically, the building sets up a two-way, welcoming relationship with its environment.

In 2008, in collaboration with Luciano Margotto, a partner at Nucleo de Arquitetura, GrupoSP won a competition to design the new headquarters of SEBRAE (a national organization that provides support to the development of small and medium enterprises) in Brasília. Alvaro Puntoni, who leads the collective, also teaches architecture at FAU-USP and the Escola da Cidade in São Paulo.

Founded in São Paulo, 2004

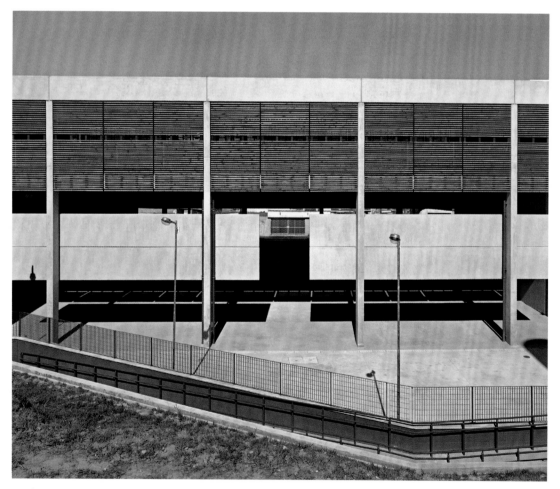

1–2.
Ataliba Leonel School,
São Paulo, 2006

3.
Vontorantim State
School, Vontorantim,
2009

1.

2.

3.

Carla Juaçaba

Based in Rio de Janeiro, where renowned architectural practices are relatively rare, Carla Juaçaba has made a name for herself both within Brazil and on the international scene. In 2012, she won the inaugural arcVision Women and Architecture Prize, an international social architecture award founded by the Italcementi Group. The prize honoured Juaçaba's work for exemplifying significant qualitative excellence and attention to the core issues of construction, such as technology, sustainability and social and cultural implications.

Following her training at the Santa Úrsula University (1999), Juaçaba developed her own practice, where she is currently engaged in both public and private projects, focusing on housing and cultural programmes. In 2000 she worked jointly with architect Mario Fraga on the Atelier House and, following that, completed a series of projects such as the Rio Bonito House (2005), the Varanda House (2007), the Minimum House (2008) and a few exhibition designs. In 2012 she collaborated with Art Director Bia Lessa on the design of the Pavilion Humanidade 2012 — a temporary exhibition hall for Rio+20, the UN conference on sustainability in Rio de Janeiro. Juaçaba imagined a multi-layered, translucent space exposed to the elements so as to remind users of their frailty in the face of nature. The architecture, which created a suspended walkway over one of Rio's main tourist sites, was primarily comprised of previously used scaffolding and was fully recyclable.

Born in Rio de Janeiro, 1976

1.

1.
Pavilion Humanidade
2012 (with Bia Lessa
and Pedro Pederneiras),
Rio de Janeiro, 2012

2–4.
Rio Bonito House, Rio
de Janeiro, 2005

2.

3.

4.

Isay Weinfeld

Isay Weinfeld is one of Brazil's leading contemporary architects. Born in São Paulo in 1952, he studied at the School of Architecture at the city's Mackenzie University and was a professor of Theory of Architecture before launching his multidisciplinary practice in 1973. Today, he is one of Brazil's most exciting contemporary architects, responsible for the elegantly minimalistic designs of numerous buildings throughout São Paulo and Rio de Janeiro, including a number of sites for the luxury hotel chain Fasano.

Weinfeld works predominantly in his home country—his career as an architect, teacher and film-maker is closely related to the city of São Paulo. Most of his projects are realized there and he has held many exhibitions and lectures focusing on the city's architectural and urban-planning problems. Recent projects include the award-winning 360° Building, the Fasano Porto Feliz, winner of Interior Design's award for best resort hotel, numerous retail spaces along the Rua Oscar Freire and stunning residential projects that showcase contemporary art. The varied nature of his work is something he encourages, saying, 'I am curious about things—I like to design things I haven't done before... I would love to design a brothel or a gas station'.

Weinfeld's architectural achievements have been recognized numerous times by the Institute of Architects of Brazil. His bookstore Livraria Da Vila won the Yellow Pencil Prize at the D&AD Awards in London in 2008 and the Spark Award in San Francisco the same year.

Born in São Paulo, 1952

1.

2.

3.

4.

1–4.
Fazenda Boa Vista
Fasano Hotel,
Porto Feliz, 2011

5–7.
Brasília House,
Brasília, 2002

5.

6.

7.

8.

9.

8
Casa Fasano,
São Paulo, 2006

9.
Casa Cubo,
São Paulo, 2011

10.
Casa Marrom,
São Paulo, 2004

11.
Equestrian Centre
Clubhouse at the
Fazenda Boa Vista,
Porto Feliz, 2012

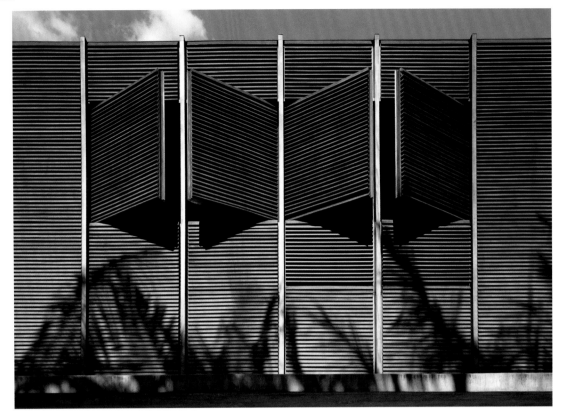

10.

11.

Brasil Arquitetura

The architectural practice Brasil Arquitetura was founded in 1979 by a trio of young and talented architects, Francisco de Paiva Fanucci, Marcelo Carvalho Ferraz and Marcelo Suzuki (Suzuki would leave the group in 1995), who worked with Lina Bo Bardi. From the start, the firm has been committed to finding architectural solutions that combine artisanal techniques and new technology across all their projects from museums, residential buildings and private houses to boutiques, restaurants and cultural centers.

The Praça das Artes (2012), a new complex in an area of São Paulo that has suffered from economic decline for decades, incorporates historic buildings alongside new volumes built in exposed concrete coloured with red pigments. Sheer walls guarantee flexibility of the internal spaces and unobstructed external spaces, while outside there are generous open spaces and new public passageways. It was shortlisted for the 2014 Designs of the Year awards by the Design Museum in London and won Building of the Year at the Icon Awards in 2013.

The Ilópolis Mill project originated as a joint initiative between private and public institutions united by their interest in the preservation of the architectural heritage of a small community in the southern state of Rio Grande do Sul. The design combines the renewal of the existing building, which is a museum, with the construction of two smaller new buildings to house a bakery and confectionery school. Exposed concrete walls generate a dialogue with the old building by using a contemporary material in its purest form.

Brasil Arquitetura is also involved in furniture and exhibition design. In 1986, they founded the 'Marcenaria Baraúna', a joinery workshop, allowing the team to control the production as well as the design of their furniture.

Founded in São Paulo, 1979

1.

1–3.
The Ilópolis Mill
Museum, Ilópolis, 2007

4.
Rodin Museum, Salvador,
2006

2.

3.

4.

UNA Arquitetos

UNA Arquitetos, founded in 1996, is an association of architects who all graduated from the FAU-USP in São Paulo. Inspired by the movement of democratic consolidation sweeping the country at the time, Cristiane Muniz, Fernando Felippe Viégas, Fábio Rago Valentim and Fernanda Barbara, along with other students, established the journal *Caramelo*, in defence of modern culture and the professionals from the dictatorship era that had been discredited, such as Paulo Mendes da Rocha. The FAU-USP building, with its covered central plaza designed by Vilanova Artigas and Carlos Cascaldi, offered the ideal refuge for a debate about the city. São Paulo was like a laboratory for reflection for the up-and-coming generations that were graduating there.

Since 1996, UNA has developed everything from schools, houses and cultural centres, to train stations, residential buildings and offices. The award-winning school they built in Campinas, north of São Paulo, is particularly interesting. The building is part of a state programme to create new schools in low-income neighbourhoods, built with a construction system involving the use of masonry and precast concrete. The small, irregular shape of the plot helped define the massive, vertical presence of the building, which stands out in the rolling landscape of fields and low-rise apartment blocks. Sixteen classrooms are distributed on two floors above the patio and a multi-use indoor sports hall crowns the building with a triple-height ceiling.

UNA has received several awards for their projects including the Carlos Milan prize, awarded by the Institute of Architects of Brazil in 2008 for the New Railroad Station of Piqueri.

Founded in São Paulo, 1996

1.

1.
School in Campinas,
Campinas, 2004

2–3.
House in Curitiba,
Curitiba, 2004

4.
House in Joanópolis,
Joanópolis, 2005

2.

3.

4.

Erika Verzutti

Marcius Galan

Jonathas de Andrade

Cinthia Marcelle

Rosângela Rennó

Rodrigo Matheus

Paulo Nazareth

Renata Lucas

Rivane Neuenschwander

Alexandre da Cunha

Kiki Mazzucchelli

art

Writer and polemicist Oswald de Andrade's seminal *Manifesto Antropófago* (Anthropophagous Manifesto, *Revista de Antropofagia*, 1928) marked a defining moment in the development of Modernism in Brazil. This influential text conceptualized the affirmation of a Brazilian cultural identity by employing the cannibalistic rituals of the native Tupinambá Indians as a metaphor for the cultural absorption and re-articulation of foreign influences to create something new and truly Brazilian. Since the 1920s, artists associated with the first wave of Modernism in the country had started to assimilate the conceptual and formal developments of the European avant-garde, with many of them having spent time studying or working abroad, particularly in Paris.

Andrade's visionary theorization of the hybrid character of Brazilian modernity (which developed the idea of a symbolic artistic practice that incorporated the values of the 'other' through 'consumption') became an important reference point for discussions around notions of cultural identity in the country. Crucially, it established the idea that it was possible—and indeed necessary—to create a modernity that, in spite of borrowing elements from the European model, was fundamentally distinct from it. The first Brazilian avant-garde experiments—mainly characterized by Cubist or Expressionist influences—were quite timid in comparison with the multifaceted production of the Dada or Surrealist groups that had emerged before them, but were nonetheless fundamental in breaking with the hitherto dominant Eurocentric academicism and in paving the way for the development of a home-grown modern aesthetic.

In the first half of the last century, Brazil was still taking its first steps in the transition from a rural, semi-feudal economy to an industrialized system that would see the emergence of an expanding middle class in growing urban centres. Against this provincial setting, modern art was undoubtedly the privilege of a few affluent individuals, and the exhibitions, salons and events organized during this period were largely one-off or short-lived initiatives supported by a small community of artists and patrons keen on defying the prevailing conservatism of the rural elites. However, the industrialization surge that took over the country by the mid-century provoked radical changes in the art circuit. Following the stock market crash of 1929, and the subsequent decline in power of Brazil's landed oligarchs, the country was swept by an ideology of progress through the modernization of old economic and social structures. Some members of the new entrepreneurial elite soon realized that it was also fundamental to foster artistic practices that reflected this progressive drive, creating the country's first modern institutions: the São Paulo Art Museum (MASP, 1947), which featured the greatest collection of old European masters in Latin America and a groundbreaking multidisciplinary education and events programme; and the first Museums of Modern Art (MAM) in São Paulo and Rio de Janeiro (1948), both inspired by the New York MoMA and supported by donations of modern European and American works by magnate Nelson Rockefeller, who also acted as a close advisor.

At the beginning of the following decade, industrialist Francisco (Ciccillo) Matarazzo Sobrinho, founder of MAM São Paulo, started another even more ambitious enterprise that would have a tremendous impact on the local circuit. When the first edition of the São Paulo Biennial took place, in 1951, it was the second event of its kind in the world, preceded only by the Venice Biennale (1895), which served as its model. The Brazilian public was finally able to experience the main artistic movements of the century on national soil and in an unprecedented systematic manner. During its first years, the Biennial presented an impressive array of comprehensive exhibitions covering

1.
Box Bolide 12
'archeologic',
Hélio Oiticica,
1964–65

2.
Desvio Para o Vermelho,
Cildo Meireles,
1967–1984, Inhotim

1.

2.

avant-garde themes including Cubism, Futurism and Neo-Plasticism, as well as a series of solo shows by renowned artists such as Calder, Chagall, Klee, Mondrian, Munch and many others. Sixty decades later, having undergone many structural changes over the years, the São Paulo Biennial continues to be one of the main platforms for showcasing international art in the country.

With a new museum and exhibition infrastructure in place, together with a booming economy, the following years marked a kind of golden age for the arts in the country, spawning a new wave of late Modernism in the 1950s and 1960s. While most artists associated with the 1920s Modern movement, such as Tarsila do Amaral or Emiliano Di Cavalcanti, were primarily concerned about issues of national identity that were explored through experiments in figuration, the emerging generation eagerly embraced abstraction. Constructivist tendencies became the main reference for a group of practitioners in Rio de Janeiro and São Paulo who today are considered key figures in Brazilian art, among them Hélio Oiticica and Lygia Clark. The term Concrete Art initially encompassed a wide range of approaches that drew on the legacy of geometric abstraction, but later became divided—with São Paulo artists maintaining a more dogmatic approach while artists in Rio de Janeiro used a more intuitive technique. The rift between the two groups led to the emergence of the Neo-Concrete movement. This new expressive space emphasized the viewer's experience of the art object, often requiring his or her participation in order to activate the work, as with Clark's famous *Bichos* (Beasts, 1960–3), a series of small sculptures formed by hinged metal plates that could be manipulated by the public, or Oiticica's *Bólides* (Fireballs, 1963–9)—structures made with cheap everyday materials often filled with pigments, stones and fabric that were also meant to be handled. Due to the radically innovative character of its proposal, breaking from the idea of the passive contemplation of artwork and seeking to reconnect art and life, Neo-Concretism is considered a turning point from modern to contemporary art in Brazil.

However, the optimism that characterized the country's modernization for over a decade would be suddenly halted by a military coup in 1964, bringing a dictatorship that would remain in power for the next twenty years. The situation intensified in 1968, when the military regime issued the AI-5, a bill that suspended several political rights and resulted in an increasing number of arbitrary incarcerations as well as widespread torture and censorship. Many artists produced works that responded directly to the current situation, at the same time as continuing to pursue aesthetic innovation. Paradoxically, repression may have contributed to the emergence of groundbreaking dematerialized or ephemeral practices, as these were harder to trace by the regime's censors. In 1969, Artur Barrio presented his first *Trouxas Ensaguentadas* (Bloody Bundles) at the Museum of Modern Art in Rio de Janeiro—works made with materials such as cement, bones, cotton wool and animal flesh wrapped together in newspaper or cloth—which were later scattered on the streets as part of his *Situações* (Situations) series. The following year, Cildo Meireles started his series of *Inserções em Circuitos Ideológicos* (Insertions into Ideological Circuits), where he famously applied subversive slogans such as 'Yankees go home!' on recyclable Coca-Cola bottles or stamped bank notes with political messages, subsequently putting them back into circulation. As new conceptual approaches started to emerge, the artists formerly associated with Neo-Concretism also began to radicalize the experimental processes they had initiated earlier in the decade: Lygia Clark's work became increasingly dematerialized and unstable in an investigation of internal psychological space, while Oiticica turned his attention to the external social space.

Under the repressive circumstances created by the dictatorship, several artists opted—or in some cases were even forced—to go into exile, with many remaining abroad for extended periods. Although the disruption caused by the new political regime did not completely halt artistic activities in the country, it certainly interrupted the process of the establishment of a stronger art circuit envisioned a decade earlier. The dictatorial regime officially came to an end in 1985, but it would still take another ten years for Brazilian art to gather significant momentum and become disseminated beyond national borders.

In 1984, an exhibition organized at the Escola de Artes Visuais do Parque Lage, in Rio de Janeiro, showcased works from more than 100 emerging artists. The exhibition, entitled *Como vai você, geração 80?* (How are you doing, people of the 1980s?), did not propose a specific curatorial remit, but instead, was a snapshot of the latest artistic manifestations taking place in the country at that particular moment. A large number of the participating artists shared a renewed interest in painting, exploring its material qualities both in abstract and figurative works. Painting became the predominant medium of the decade, and an art market was gradually being formed around this more commercially viable production.

Importantly, the gradual establishment of a local gallery circuit over the next few years played a decisive role in what is commonly referred to as the process of internationalization of Brazilian art in the 1990s. The presence of pioneering dealers such as Thomas Cohn, Luisa Strina and Marcantonio Vilaça in major art fairs in America and Europe helped to give visibility to a number of Brazilian artists in the northern hemisphere. At the same time, Western academics, curators and museum directors were also beginning to turn their attention to artistic production outside hegemonic countries. This heightened interest and exposure resulted in the progressive inclusion of artists such as Tunga—whose unique sculptural pieces are charged with symbolic meanings—in prominent institutional exhibitions abroad. His work had been showcased at the Venice Biennale in 1982, but over the next decade he would exhibit at MoMA, in New York (1993) and Documenta, in Kassel (1997), among others. With a work that combines the country's constructive legacy with a conceptual approach, young artist Jac Leirner was also among the first Brazilians to establish an international career, having taken part at the Venice Biennale (1990) and at Documenta (1991).

The decade also saw the first signs of the absorption of Neo-Concretism in Western art historiography. In 1992, the Witte de With, in Rotterdam, presented Hélio Oiticica's first retrospective, which later toured to Paris, Barcelona, Lisbon and Minneapolis, finally arriving at the Centro Cultural Hélio Oiticica, in Rio de Janeiro, in 1996. A major survey of Lygia Clark's work was organized by the Fundació Antoni Tàpies in 1997, later travelling to Marseille, Porto and Brussels. As well as bringing this production to new audiences, both shows played an important role in the dissemination of knowledge about the late Brazilian avant-garde through the publication of comprehensive catalogues in foreign languages, making it accessible for the first time to international curators and scholars.

Another key moment in the dissemination of Brazilian art took place within the country at the end of the decade. The twenty-fourth edition of the São Paulo Biennial (1998), curated by Paulo Herkenhoff, took Oswald de Andrade's notion of *antropofagia* (cannibalism) as its starting point. In a bold move, Herkenhoff proposed to reflect on international art from the viewpoint of a local theoretical idea. His intentions were particularly successful in the

Biennial's *Núcleo Histórico* section, with its display strategy of 'contamination', where historic masterpieces were shown side by side with contemporary works. Contemporary Brazilian art was also extremely well represented, including several artists that were still relatively unknown outside the country and who today are among the most prominent: Beatriz Milhazes, with her carefully layered paintings populated by colourful decorative motifs; Ernesto Neto, whose unique installations of drop-like volumes filled with a variety of spices ingeniously update Neo-Concrete ideas; and Adriana Varejão, who revisits and reinterprets Brazil's history in paintings and installations that expose the violence of its colonial past.

3.
À Luz de Dois Mundos,
Tunga, 2010, Louvre
Gallery, Paris

The twenty-first century has seen contemporary Brazilian art assert its place in the international arena. Within this relatively short period, some of the most renowned institutions in Europe and the US have held surveys of established Brazilian artists and Brazilian art has been chosen as the theme of several group exhibitions. This widespread international presence gave rise to a new phenomenon acknowledged by curator Adriano Pedrosa in the thirty-first edition of *Panorama da Arte Brasileira* (2009), a biennial survey of national art organized by the Museum of Modern Art in São Paulo. Inverting *antropofagia*'s equation, Pedrosa organized an exhibition presenting works by emerging foreign artists who 'cannibalize' Brazilian culture by borrowing and reprocessing elements of modern art and architecture, concrete poetry, bossa nova and *Tropicália*. If twenty years ago interest in Brazilian art was restricted to a small group of collectors and professionals, now it is disseminated to the point of influencing artists worldwide.

Concurrently with significant changes in the international scenario, there were important developments within the Brazilian circuit. The first two decades of the twenty-first century witnessed the emergence of several art centres across different parts of the country. Prior to that, art professionals often sought to relocate either to Rio de Janeiro or São Paulo in order to find work, but the recent reshaping or creation of new institutions and programmes across other regions, as well as the resulting increased professionalism of local milieus, means that the art circuit is now beginning to reflect the complex, multilayered character of Brazilian contemporary art production. The popularization of digital technologies and increasingly affordable air travel have also contributed to reducing the geographical isolation of areas thousands of kilometres away from the country's two main economic centres. In this process, not only did a new generation of artists from outside the hegemonic Rio de Janeiro-São Paulo hub become inserted into the national circuit, but also a body of works by mature local practitioners from these regions, previously off the radar, began to be 'rediscovered', prompting a revision of national art historical narratives of the post-1960s period.

Porto Alegre, in southern Brazil, has hosted the Mercosul Biennial since 1996, 'as an attempt by business and artistic leaders to establish their city as an alternative to the Rio de Janeiro/São Paulo cultural axis and the dominance of the São Paulo Biennial', according to the Mercosul website. With a focus on Latin American art—unlike the internationalist approach of its São Paulo counterpart—the Mercosul Biennial only managed to assert its presence and significance in its sixth edition (2007) curated by Gabriel Pérez-Barreiro, whose exhibition title, *The Third Bank of the River,* was taken from a short story by Brazilian writer Guimarães Rosa. An innovative education programme, devised by Uruguayan artist Luis Camnitzer, which included a series of actions aimed at empowering and including the audience, was one of the distinctive features of the exhibition. Pérez-Barreiro's proposal achieved international resonance

3.

and, for the first time, the Mercosul Biennial became a 'must-see' event in the global art professional's agenda. In the following years, curatorial teams led by prominent chief curators with wide international experience—such as the Colombian José Roca and the Mexican Sofía Hernandez Chong Cuy—have managed to produce engaging, thought-provoking exhibitions that promote a reflection on global art from a Latin American perspective, thus establishing Porto Alegre as an important art destination in the country.

Further north in the coastal city of Recife, a prolific contemporary art scene began to emerge in the early 2000s, fostered by the availability of extra state funding. Curator and researcher, Moacir dos Anjos, played a pivotal role in this process during his term as director of Museu de Arte Moderna Aloísio Magalhães (MAMAM) (2001–6), when he organized a series of solo exhibitions by established contemporary Brazilian artists—among them Antonio Dias, Artur Barrio, Nelson Leirner, Ernesto Neto and Rivane Neuenschwander—creating the opportunity for a young generation of art professionals to gain first-hand experience of works by some of the most significant practitioners in the country.

Equally important in the development of Recife's local art scene is the week-long, open-call festival SPA das Artes, created in 2002, which comprises a series of events such as performances, workshops and artistic interventions across the city. Self-organized initiatives by young artists and curators, such as conferences, debates and independent magazines also contributed to the dissemination of artistic and critical research from the region to a wider Brazilian audience. Within the context of a practically non-existent local market, the Recife art scene largely relies on public funding, and is therefore subjected to the continuous fluctuations of governmental investment in the arts. However, over the past two decades, the city has established itself as a hub for artistic practices in the prolific northeastern region of the country. It has also produced some of the most interesting artists of the new generation, such as Jonathas de Andrade and Rodrigo Braga, as well as curators, writers and researchers that have contributed immensely to the expansion of traditional Brazilian art historiography (largely focused on the Rio de Janeiro-São Paulo axis) through the study of local ground-breaking practises fostered by artists from previous generations, such as Montez Magno and Paulo Bruscky.

Finally, another example of the decentralization of Brazilian art over the last twenty years can be found in the city of Belo Horizonte, in the inland state of Minas Gerais. One of the most significant projects initiated in the city during this period was an artist residency scheme at the Museu de Arte da Pampulha (MAP), an elegant building, formerly a casino, designed by architect Oscar Niemeyer as part of the Pampulha Architectural Complex (1943). Created in 2002, the *Bolsa Pampulha* (Pampulha Grant) updated and expanded the model of the existing art salon promoted by the museum into a biennial open-call, fully funded, year-long residency programme for emerging Brazilian artists. This pioneering model in the country gives the unique opportunity for artists to delve into their practice for a whole year while receiving periodical tutorials from the members of the board, formed by renowned curators and academics on a rotational basis. To date, *Bolsa Pampulha* has helped to foster the careers of some of the most prominent young artists in the country including Cinthia Marcelle, Matheus Rocha-Pitta, Rodrigo Matheus, Sara Ramo and many others who, today, are internationally recognized.

Opened in the suburbs of Belo Horizonte in 2006, the Instituto Cultural Inhotim had a great impact on the internal art circuit, establishing a new paradigm for the presentation of Brazilian art within Brazil and capturing the imagination of visitors worldwide. Created by art collector and iron-ore magnate Bernardo Paz, Inhotim is an open-air contemporary art museum and botanical garden currently occupying a beautiful landscaped area spread across approximately 100 hectares (247 acres) in the remote municipality of Brumadinho. A former collector of modern Brazilian art, Paz started to turn his attention to artists from his own generation — such as Tunga, Cildo Meireles and Miguel Rio Branco — in the late 1990s, and soon identified the need to create an institution capable of collecting and permanently displaying the often large-scale installations made by these artists, which by then were either under-represented in public collections or sitting in storage. Virtually unconstrained by spatial limitations, artists are often invited to develop ambitious projects for the site, and purpose-built pavilions are erected to house acquired or newly commissioned works.

Being a private institution, Inhotim does not have the obligation to build a collection according to the same parameters as public museums, which acquire works from a wide range of practitioners. On the contrary, it acquires a small number of artists in depth, incorporating several works by the same authors in a collection that aims to reflect the breadth of their trajectories. Whole pavilions are dedicated to the works of a single artist, and there are custom-built spaces for key historical works, allowing them to be on permanent display for the first time in the country's history.

It is noteworthy that Inhotim also collects international art, which is shown alongside its Brazilian counterparts, therefore creating interesting dialogues between these productions. Until very recently, the São Paulo Biennial was practically the only platform for systematically showing international art in the country, although since the mid-2000s museums and cultural centres such as MAM-SP, Pinacoteca do Estado and Centro Cultural Banco do Brasil have been increasingly promoting exhibitions of non-Brazilian artists. Still, public institutions currently do not have a policy of acquiring international art, and by widening its geographical scope, the Inhotim collection provides a unique opportunity for the public to experience contemporary Brazilian art in relation to works by significant global names. At a moment when discussions around the notion of internationalism are at the forefront of the artistic debate, Inhotim became an important laboratory for considering Brazilian production beyond a national agenda.

The impressive growth of the Brazilian art circuit in the past decade coincided with the country's first period of sustained economic stability since the pre-dictatorship era. It also took place in parallel to an increasing internationalization of the global art scene and the emergence of new art centres, residency programmes and biennials across Asia, Eastern Europe and the Middle East. Under these favourable conditions, a number of galleries representing a brand new generation of artists emerged in Rio de Janeiro and São Paulo. However, in the institutional arena the situation was not quite so positive. Important public museums such as MASP and MAC-USP in São Paulo or the MAM in Rio de Janeiro, which hold some of the country's most important collections, suffer from a chronic lack of funding. The precarious financial situation of these museums means they are unable to update their collections through the acquisition of a significant number of contemporary works or to carry out a long-term exhibition and education programme. Under Brazil's current corporate tax exemption schemes, most companies have chosen to create their own cultural centres instead of contributing to public institutions. Venues created by the corporate sector — such as Centro Cultural Banco do Brasil or Itaú Cultural — operate without an artistic director or an in-house curatorial team, presenting a wide range of disconnected exhibitions of

4.

4.
Galeria True Rouge,
Inhotim Contemporary
Art Institute

5.
Galeria Adriana
Varejao, Inhotim
Contemporary Art
Institute

6.
Invenção da Cor,
Penetrável Magic Square
No. 5, De luxe, Helio
Oiticica, 1977, Inhotim
Contemporary Art
Institute

5.

6.

variable quality. Also benefitting from a tax law, SESC is a non-profit private entity, which offers a range of cultural activities, health services and sports facilities at a low cost across all Brazilian states. A leading financer of culture in the country, it has a particularly strong focus on the arts in the state of São Paulo, under the regional directorship of Danilo Miranda, hosting ambitious events such as the Videobrasil International Festival since 1992.

Brazilian art entered the second decade of the twenty-first century with unprecedented international recognition, a strong internal market and a few mature institutions, but there is still a lot to be done. While new initiatives such as the creation of Museu de Arte do Rio (MAR) — a partnership between the Mayor of Rio and a private foundation under the artistic direction of renowned curator Paulo Herkenhoff — contribute to the diversification of the local scene, existing museums holding valuable collections still need to reach a higher level of professionalism. As the work of young Brazilians increasingly circulates abroad, it would also be interesting to see more institutional exhibitions of international artists in Brazil, currently largely restricted to monographic shows of super-established names or solo presentations and occasional group exhibitions in commercial galleries and art fairs. Furthermore, the current imbalance between the commercial and institutional sectors creates a situation in which artists have few opportunities to work on more experimental or long-term projects that are usually commissioned by non-profit institutions.

Since 2010, Brazil has been experiencing an economic slowdown, which, in 2013, was followed by a wave of protests against corruption and the generalized inefficiency of public services. Whether or not Brazil will be hit by the crisis that has been afflicting North American and European nations since 2008 still remains to be seen. Brazilians had been producing art of outstanding quality in adverse conditions for a long time before the recent period of democratic and economic stability, and will undoubtedly continue to do so. Indeed, its future involves challenging structural changes, but also many positive prospects. One thing is certain: Brazilian art is no longer a footnote to historical narratives of contemporary art — it has become one of its most fundamental elements.

Erika Verzutti

Erika Verzutti's sculptures combine a wide range of mundane and erudite references in organic compositions. Often cast in bronze or concrete, these works are characterized by their crooked, unstable appearance, sometimes appearing as if they are on the verge of collapsing. Furthermore, evidence of the artistic technique such as dents, fingerprints and splashes of paint, are often maintained, attesting to the impossibility of fully controlling the art-making process.

Verzutti's repertoire includes recurring images of natural elements such as fruits or vegetables, as well as artistic tools like paintbrushes and paint mixing trays that are put together in seemingly precarious arrangements. Historical artworks are frequently a source of inspiration: Picasso's famous bull's head is given a renewed existence in *Ox* (2008), while Tarsila do Amaral's strange Loch Ness monster-like figure as depicted in *Sol Poente* (Setting Sun, 1929) takes on a three-dimensional existence in *Tarsila com Laranja* (Tarsila with Orange, 2011). Verzutti usually produces series of works that comprise a coherent exploration of specific themes and their formal and semantic possibilities. In the *Brasília* series (2010–12), for instance, she applies various incisions and colours to a jackfruit cast in bronze, creating works such as *Brasília Cinema* (2010), *Brasília Spoon* (2012) and *Brasília TV* (2011).

Born in São Paulo, 1971

1.

1.
Selected works, Galeria
Fortes Vilaça, 2011

2.
Missionary, 2011

3.
Tortoise, 2012

4.
Beijo, 2011

5.
Dino Pot, 2012

2.

3.

4.

5.

Marcius Galan

Marcius Galan's objects, sculptures and installations bring together the abstract geometric and conceptual legacies that have recurrently appeared in Brazilian art practices over the past fifty years. Characterized by their minimalist aesthetics and impeccable finish, his works often investigate the gap between the scientific representation of the world — through geometry or mathematics — and lived experience.

Galan constantly plays with the inherent qualities and the visual appearance of materials: in his series *Isolantes* (*Isolating*, 2008–ongoing) a yellow ribbon is carefully folded, hanging, seemingly loosely, from the wall or tied around a set of bricks; however, upon closer inspection it becomes apparent that these

ribbons are made of solid metal. This illusory quality is even more pronounced in installations such as *Three Sections* (2012), where an entire room is covered with paint, wax and light filters to create the impression that the room is sectioned by three green-tinted panes of glass.

Born in Indianapolis, 1972

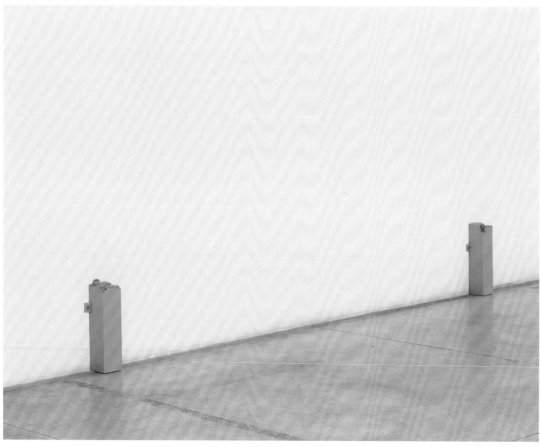

1.
Duas Paralelas Que
Não Se Encontram No
Infinito (Two Parallels
Which Do Not Meet In
Infinity), 2004

2.
Three Sections, 2011

3.
Uri Geller, 2011

4.
Área Comúm
(Common Area), 2008

1.

2.

3.

4.

5.

5.
Immobile, 2013

6.
Diagrama, 2013

7.
Ponto Em Escala Real
(Point In Real Scale),
2010

6.

7.

Jonathas de Andrade

Working across photography, installation and film, Jonathas de Andrade's art focuses on Brazil's social history and its effects on contemporary behaviours and class relations. Andrade often borrows existing documents and texts, combining them with new elements to create fictional and subjective narratives. In *Ressaca Tropical* (Tropical Hangover, 2009), the artist appropriated a diary salvaged from a rubbish tip, written in the 1970s by an anonymous author who diligently narrated his sexual adventures in the city of Recife. The entries are shown on separate pages presented as a sequence on the gallery walls and displayed alongside photographs from public and private archives, as well as new images produced by the artist, mostly depicting Recife's urban transformations over the past 50 years.

In *Museu do Homem do Nordeste* (Museum of the Northeastern Man, 2013), Andrade takes the homonymous ethnographic institution created by sociologist Gilberto Freyre in Recife as a starting point. For this project, after placing advertisements in local newspapers, Andrade recruited several working class men and used their portraits to illustrate fictional posters for the museum.

Born in Maceió, 1982

1.

68

6. Pay attention to the point! Bananas will go from being caramelised to a dense, dark and very sugary stage. Taste them now. And keep on tasting them. You need to get the perfect color and use your hand to feel the texture which brings out the full flavor. But beware! The secret is not to let this moment slip away.

6. Attention à la cuisson ! Les bananes passeront d'un état caramélisé à une texture dure, foncée et très sucrée. Goûtez à ce moment-là. Continuez à goûter de temps en temps. Il faut atteindre la couleur parfaite et sentir la texture qui fasse ressortir la pureté du goût. Mais attention ! Le secret est justement de ne pas laisser ce moment vous échapper.

7. DEIXE DESCANSAR 8. DESPEJE AINDA QUENTE EM RECIPIENTE LISO, FORRADO DE AÇÚCAR 9. QUANTO MAIS CONSISTENTE CORTE, E REPARTA EM PEDACINHOS 10. BANHE-OS NO AÇÚCAR. DEPOIS EMBALE EM PAPEL TRANSPARENTE.
11. SIRVA E DELICIE-SE !

7. Let it sit. 8. Pour it when still hot into a receptacle.
9. This, lined with sugar.
10. Cover with the sugar.
Afterwards wrap in transparent paper.
11. Serve and taste how delightful they are!

7. Laissez reposer. 8. Versez le contenu encore chaud dans un récipient lisse, recouvert de sucre.
9. Après avoir durci, coupez le tout en petits morceaux.
10. Passez-les dans le sucre. Puis emballez-les dans du papier transparent.
11. Servez et régalez-vous !

2.

3.

1–2.
40 Nego Bom é um Real
(40 Black Candies for
R$1), 2013

3–4.
Museu do Homem do
Nordeste (Museum of
the Northeastern Man)
exhibition, 2013

4.

Cinthia Marcelle

Cinthia Marcelle's work is characterized by the allegorical reorganization of everyday situations, often transforming them into unexpected, purposeless events. *Unus Mundus* (2004–8) consisted of a series of actions documented in video, recorded with a single fixed camera from an aerial perspective. The series included *Confronto* (*Confrontation*, 2005), which depicted street fire jugglers at a crossroad in the centre of Belo Horizonte gradually interrupting the flow of traffic, sparking anger among motorists. The work suggests ideas of resistance within society, but also attests to the emergence of conflict and aggressiveness in human relations.

475 Volver (2009) is a video showing a JCB digging itself deeper and deeper into the freshly deforested red soil of central Brazil in the shape of an infinity loop. *Fonte 193* (Fountain 193, 2007) shows a fire engine that continuously drives around in a circle into the centre of which it pours water, creating a perfect drawing on the land, a seemingly pointless action that produces the image of a fountain in reverse. Another body of works includes photographs depicting characters that are partially merged with rural or urban landscapes, like the hooded white horse against the red-tinted countryside soil (*The Speaker*, 2004), or the artist herself posing in front of a building in Cape Town wearing an outfit that camouflages her against the facade (*Cape Town*, 2003).

Born in Belo Horizonte, 1974

1.
O Conversador
(The Speaker), 2005

2.
O Cosmopolita
(The Cosmopolitan),
2011

3.
O Conto Fantástico
(The Fantastic Story),
2012

4.
O Colecionador
(The Collector), 2011

5.
Untitled from 'Com
Contra des Desde'
series, 2011

6.
See to be Seen
exhibition, 2011

1.

2.

3.

4.

5.   6.

Rosângela Rennó

Known as the photographer who does not take pictures, Rosângela Rennó has been developing a solid body of works over the last twenty-five years. With a unique conceptual approach to photography, Rennó is renowned for her appropriation of existing, non-artistic photographic archives, producing beautifully constructed and politically charged works that investigate the conditions and ethics of image production in different contexts. Among her most celebrated series is *Vulgo* (1998–9), where she presented portraits taken from the archive of the São Paulo Penitentiary Museum, examining the use of photography as a tool for control and power. The original negatives were produced between 1920 and 1940, when the prison's department of psychiatric criminology intended to classify and identify inmates through their singular physical characteristics. They depict details such as the back of their necks or the top of their heads, seeking to establish a scientific relationship between certain typologies and criminal behaviours.

In her *Série Vermelha (Militares)* (Red Series [Military], 2001), Rennó collected bourgeois family portraits from different countries (Brazil, USA, Germany, Russia and others) featuring men and children wearing military uniform. These images are layered with a red filter, transforming them into ghostly memories of latent violence in society.

Born in Belo Horizonte, 1962

1.

2.

3.

1.
Febre do Cerrado
(Savanna Fever), 2008

2.
Lote 16 Apagamento por
Empilhamento do Projeto
Menos-Valia (Leilão)
(Lot 16 Erasure by
Stacking from Minus-
Value [Auction]
Project), 2010

3.
Paula Trope, formato
9 x 12, from the 'A
Última Foto' (The Last
Photo) project, 2006

4.
Untitled (Tattoo 6A and
6B), 1997

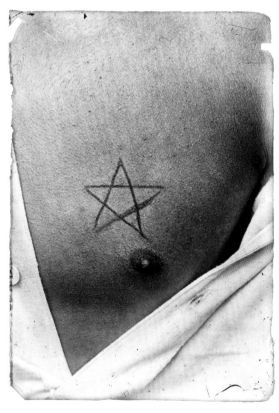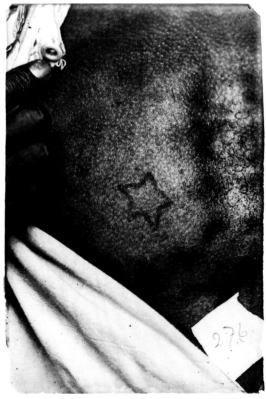

4.

Rodrigo Matheus

Rodrigo Matheus's sculptural pieces, installations and collages explore the formal and symbolic possibilities of everyday objects and found materials. These elements are removed from their original context, combined and reconfigured into surprisingly formal arrangements in order to take on new meanings. For a series of wall-based works developed throughout 2013, Matheus acquired several documents dating from the early-twentieth century that record different types of commercial transactions between Brazil and England. These were juxtaposed within intricate compositions along with other elements such as artificial plants, postcards of tropical beaches, shells and fishing baits, producing a clash of historical and contemporary references.

Matheus usually chooses his objects and materials in relation to the specific use and meaning they have in different societies. The process of displacement and reconfiguration within the gallery context underscores certain aspirations, behaviours and social practices, which are articulated in pieces characterized by a dry sense of humour.

Born in São Paulo, 1974

1.
Ceiling Rose, 2014

2.
Eclipse, 2012

1.

2.

3.

4.

5.

Paulo Nazareth

Paulo Nazareth's works reclaim the experimental conceptualism of the 1970s in order to investigate the cultural, economic and social conditions behind the marginalization of black and indigenous people in Latin American countries. A charismatic figure, the artist draws on his own mixed heritage in his actions, performances, photographs and texts produced during his constant peregrinations across the world. In an early action staged at a central square in Mumbai in 2006, Nazareth stood alongside a sign offering passers-by one rupee if they succeeded in guessing his country of origin. A small crowd soon formed, but after several unsuccessful attempts a policeman dispersed the mob.

Nazareth rose to prominence in the international scene with the project *Notícia de América* (News from America, 2011–12), where he embarked on a trip, mainly by foot, through more than fifteen countries in Latin America before reaching the United States. Among the several works produced during this pilgrimage is a series of photographs entitled *Cara de Índio* (Indigenous Faces), in which he photographed himself next to people from different indigenous backgrounds, highlighting the vast array of heterogeneous physical characteristics that are encompassed by the term 'indigenous'.

Playing with preconceived notions of identity in a humorous manner, Nazareth is one of the few voices to tackle racial issues in Brazilian contemporary art.

Born in Governador Valadares, 1977

1.

2.

1.
Pneu, 2012

2.
Coleção Produtos de
Genocídio, 2013

3.
Unstable Territory,
Florence, Italy, 2013

4.
Todos Os Santos da
Minha Mãe (My Mother's
Saints), 2013

3.

4.

Renata Lucas

Renata Lucas's work consists mainly of site-specific interventions on public or architectural areas that alter, displace or reconfigure the space in order to produce new experiences of perception. These interventions are usually temporary, momentarily highlighting the ways in which behaviours are determined by the built environment around us.

In one of her early works, *Crossing* (2003), Lucas covered a road junction in Rio de Janeiro with plywood, a simple but effective gesture that had a strong visual impact but also played on other senses, as it affected the sound of the passing cars. In 2010, Lucas made a circular incision on the gallery floor at KW Institute for Contemporary Art, in Berlin, which was split in half by the position of the wall. The floor became a revolving surface, which could be rotated by visitors with their feet, revealing the grassed external half of the circle.

In *The Resident* (2007), Lucas modified the facade of a residency space in London, covering its surface with traditional terracotta bricks and creating a recessed area featuring a working radiator where passers-by could momentarily escape from the cold.

Born in Ribeirão Preto, 1971

1.

2.

1.
Crossing, 2003

2.
Prototype for a Sliding
Ground, 2009

3.
The Resident, 2007

4.
Kunst-Werke, 2010

3.

4.

Rivane Neuenschwander

Working across a wide range of media, Rivane Neuenschwander is renowned for creating installations that often involve the participation of the public. In *I Wish Your Wish* (2003) hundreds of the colourful silk ribbons traditionally worn around the wrists of Brazilians—who believe that their wishes are granted when the ribbons wear away and fall off—were printed with wishes from previous visitors and hung from the gallery walls. The public were encouraged to remove a ribbon and tie it to their wrist, replacing it with a new wish written on a piece of paper.

Language also plays a central role in Neuenschwander's work, such as in *Story of an Other* (2005), where she presented a set of modified typewriters whose letter keys had been replaced by symbols and dots. Visitors were invited to type, finding new ways of communicating, and their messages were displayed in the installation. A keen observer of everyday life, the artist often takes on seemingly insignificant gestures as inspiration for her projects.

Born in Belo Horizonte, 1967

1.

1.
Involuntary Sculptures
(Speech Acts),2001—2010
[A series of objects
made by anonymous
people collected from
bars and restaurants]

2—4.
Untitled (Anonymous
Furniture, Sao
Joaquim), 2013
[Reproductions
of anonymously
designed seats made
by professional
carpenters]

2.

3.

4.

5.

5.
[...], 2005

6.
Globes, 2003 [balls
of various sizes
representing the flags
of all the nations in
the world, as of 2003]

7.
I Wish Your Wish, 2003

6.

7.

Alexandre da Cunha

Alexandre da Cunha's work is characterized by the appropriation of objects, materials and citations from traditionally distinct registers that are transformed through a process of collage. This operation usually begins with everyday items such as mops, towels or toilet plungers, which are appropriated, recombined and finally re-inserted into a new hierarchy of value. By bringing such objects into the universe of art, the artist removes their original function, at the same time raising questions related to value, circulation and intention.

In many cases, he also alludes to specific styles or movements recognized by official Western Art History, thus creating — with (self)-critical humour — a hierarchical short-circuit. *Platinum Column* (2006), a sculpture made from stacked kitchen bowls, evokes Brancusi's *Endless Column*, while in the series *Deck Painting* (2005– ongoing) the stripped canvas taken from beach chairs is put on stretchers, referencing Daniel Buren's paintings.

Having been based in London for over a decade, Da Cunha often plays with Brazil's exotic image as projected by foreigners, as in the series *Seascapes (Flags)* (2008), where photographs of idyllic tropical beaches are combined with geometrical patterns.

Born in Rio de Janeiro, 1969

1.

1.
Public Sculpture
(Pouff 1), 2008

2.
Kentucky (Drop), 2011

3.
Bust, 2012

2.

3.

Carlos Motta

Fernando Prado

Jader Almeida

Marcelo Rosenbaum

OVO

Domingos Tótora

Zanini de Zanine

Campana Brothers

Mara Gama

design

Brazil is creating more design, and it is creating better design. It is experimenting with form and improving technical quality, it is incorporating artisanal traditions, revisiting the richness of its Modernist past and generating more interest and greater reception abroad. This is the time for Brazilian design.

1.
Bowl Chair, Lina Bo
Bardi, 1951

Over the last ten years, names such as Jader Almeida, Zanini de Zanine, Fernando Prado and Gerson de Oliveira & Luciana Martins (of OVO) have explored diverse aesthetic approaches and technically improved their production in furniture, lighting and product design, today standing alongside Brazil's best-known designers such as Carlos Motta and the Campana brothers as international figures. The growth of the country's design scene is evident in the countless editorials, television shows and websites dedicated to the subject, and the visibility of Brazilian designers in new editions of reference books, historical essays, magazines and programmes has increased significantly over the past decade. Internally, the burgeoning luxury market has seen great advances in terms of technical excellence and aesthetic diversity, but the real challenge for Brazilian design is to offer new solutions that suit both the local, urgent needs of the majority of the population and their budgets — to truly enter the homes and daily lives of the everyday Brazilian.

The rise of design education in Brazil over recent years has been remarkable: currently, there are around 450 technical undergraduate courses related strictly to furniture and product design throughout the country, as well as ten Masters programmes and at least three doctoral programmes. The vast majority of these have been running for less than ten years. In its latest edition, in 2013, the pioneering Prêmio Design, the oldest and most important design contest in the country, organized by the Museu da Casa Brasileira (MCB), received more than 800 entries. Designers from every corner of Brazil submitted projects for all categories from construction, transportation and electronics, to lighting, furniture, textile and product design, across the two different classifications: prototypes and those ready for production.

Founded in 1986, the MCB prize was for some time the only national platform for the exhibition of new projects, but is today accompanied by nearly 20 other respected contests across the country. The Casa Brasil and MovelBrasil awards, both based in the town of Bento Gonçalves in Rio Grande do Sul, draw Brazilians from all over the country, as well as participants from other Latin American nations and even Europe, with the number of applicants consistently surpassing 1,000. Other important contests have appeared, aimed specifically at young designers and students. Projects focused on sustainability, environmental solutions and ecology have been encouraged through awards such as the Casa-Objeto Brasileiro and Planeta Casa, among others.

In the 2000s, the Brazilian design Biennials became itinerant — each time celebrated in a different state in order to disseminate design culture and lend value to regional production. In 2006, the event was in São Paulo; in 2008, Brasília; in 2010, Curitiba and in 2012, Belo Horizonte. Due to the 2014 World Cup, the next Biennial is scheduled for 2015, and will be held in Santa Catarina. The idea of focusing on distinct regions was not an isolated institutional initiative — Brazilian design already exists beyond the Rio de Janeiro-São Paulo axis, despite the powerful consumer market of these two cities — but instead a conscious decision to celebrate these new, flourishing centres of production. The development of industry in the southern part of the country, particularly in the states of Paraná, Santa Catarina and Rio Grande do Sul, changed the map of Brazilian design significantly.

1.

2.

2.
Oscar Chair, Sergio
Rodrigues, 1956

3.
Rio Chaise, Oscar
Niemeyer & Anna Maria
Niemeyer, 1978—79

3.

Part of the recent expansion of design can be attributed to the population's increased spending power, lower levels of unemployment and greater access to information and culture, afforded by decreasing inflation, economic stability, social inclusion policies and the strengthening of democracy. But Brazilian design didn't just take advantage of a growing consumer market and adapt to rising demand. Recently, there have been important changes in the way design is thought about, made and interpreted in the country.

Following their international success, brothers Humberto and Fernando Campana have become a parameter for boldness and 'Brazilianness' both within Brazil and abroad. Their work, which sits on the border between design, craftwork and art, generally involves cheap and seemingly mundane materials, and its innovative approach has influenced a generation of designers currently benefitting from the world's curiosity towards Brazil.

Foreign interest in Brazilian Modernism of the 1940s and 1950s, the golden era of Brazilian architecture, has also recently crossed into the field of furniture design, driven by a number of publications and collectors' displays of vintage and modernist pieces. One example is the show 'Brazilian Design: Modern and Contemporary Furniture', held in Berlin in 2012 and in London in 2014. Considered the largest exhibition of Brazilian design ever held in Europe, the event showcased more than 80 pieces of furniture and other objects from both the Modernist period and contemporary design. Work by iconic designers such as Lina Bo Bardi, Paulo Mendes da Rocha, Oscar Niemeyer and Sergio Rodrigues, was displayed alongside pieces by the Campanas, Carlos Motta, and OVO, amongst others. The value of Modernist design helped shed light on designers who, in their own way, continue that lineage.

Over the last ten years, production conditions have changed: new techniques, materials and machines — such as laser cutters, rapid prototyping tools, 3D and acrylic printers, resins, paints, laminates and composites — have become cheaper and more accessible, allowing greater freedom, quality control and more sophisticated finishes. With increased investment in contests and exhibitions, designers are now closer than ever to factories and in-company production teams. In turn, the furniture industry has opened up to design and designers. Many professionals have taken up issues related to social inclusion, rational use of resources and responsible consumption in their agendas. The ethics of production have been incorporated into the debate. Still, many different production methods co-exist in the country: from totally artisanal to totally industrial, as well as hybrid approaches. Artisanal craftwork and increasingly valued regional traditions are eliciting genuine interest from creators and consumers. And Brazilian designers are partly responsible for this revitalization, according to design critic Adélia Borges, who cites examples such as that of Coopa-Roca — a cooperative of residents of Rio de Janeiro's Rocinha *favela* who, since the 1980s, have supplied material to stylists — and the stories of designers such as Domingos Tótora, Renato Imbroisi and Marcelo Rosenbaum. As well as having a direct impact on the quality of artisanal production processes in the country, these designers have played the mid-field between communities and the market, contributing to communications and the strategic management of production.

The unification of design and artisanal crafts in Brazil is a recent phenomenon. In an opposite trajectory to those seen in countries such as England, Italy and Finland, where design has benefited from the artisan tradition, in Brazil, designers have traditionally tried to distance themselves from manual labour. Borges attributes the schism between artisanal work and design to the strong rationalist thinking implanted in the country's schools, ever since the Escola Superior de Design opened its doors in Rio in 1963. The notion of good universal design excluded the possibility of valuing imprecise vernacular design stemming from archaic modes of production.

Today, Brazilian design is much more accepting of its roots, and there has been an increasing trend for contemporary designers to incorporate elements of traditional production into their work. An exemplary case of this is Renato Imbroisi, who graduated in visual communication in São Paulo and has been experimenting in the field of artisanal weaving since the 1990s. In his textile pieces, Imbroisi—a staunch defender of design as a tool for social transformation—combines raw materials such as seeds, leaves, flowers and branches with his pre-woven fabrics. Over the last 25 years he has worked with communities of manual labourers with their own means of traditional textile production—from crochet, weaving and embroidery, to lace and basket-making, prioritizing popular cultural legacies and, at the same time, integrating local raw materials, technical training and forms of fair trade to improve the sustainability and responsibility of each production.

Another strong theme in contemporary Brazilian design is recycling: the re-use of offcuts, scraps, leftover materials and everyday items has become ever more popular amongst designers, as demonstrated by figures such as Rodrigo Almeida, Rodrigo Bueno and Bruno Jahara. It is also apparent in the work of Domingos Tótora. He works with a material that he has developed and perfected, mixing cardboard from discarded boxes with water and glue. With this new material, he moulds the organic, sculptural forms of his benches, utensils, containers, table mounts, chairs and decorative panels. The final treatment explores the frugality of each object and the simplicity of basic colours, and its production employs local people in the collection of recycled materials and in the manufacture and casting of pieces.

Material is particularly important in Brazilian design, and none is more popular or prevalent than wood. Wood is the obvious link between Brazilian designers throughout the last century, helping define the Brazilian-ness of design and continues to be explored in diverse ways by designers such as Carlos Motta and Jader Almeida, who take almost opposite approaches. Though the two share common influences, both strongly admiring the Modernists for example, the former uses only Brazilian woods, and seeks to minimize the interference of machinery, probing the nuances of its nature. The latter's approach to the material is to extract every bit of its physical versatility, moulding it with any technology available. In the middle ground between these two approaches lies the work of designers such as Fernando Mendes, Paulo Alves, Hugo França and Claudia Moreira Salles.

Brazilian design still has a lot of room for development, both because a large part of the country's diverse culture and way of life is still relatively unexplored, and also because, despite the variety, throughout the territory the population faces fundamental problems that remain unaddressed. There is an urgent need for housing, for the urbanization of *favelas*, for the protection of the lands and the rights of indigenous peoples. There is a need for basic sanitation, the efficient treatment of water, for waste management, supporting education and for new ways of democratizing access to health care.

The good news is that a large part of the discussions around solutions to these issues has taken design into account, and that with the desire to seek a more accessible and popular design, many of these aspects can be better explored.

4–6.
Anonymous stool designs

4.

5.

6.

Carlos Motta

Carlos Motta trained as an architect in São Paulo during the 1970s before moving to California, where he studied woodwork and discovered the pared back aesthetics of American furniture. Back in Brazil, he began to produce his own designs, looking to establish simple wooden products with an ecological approach that considered the durability of the items and the recycling of raw materials long before sustainability became an important issue.

His São Paulo Chair project in the 1980s saw his first foray into mass production. The successful sales of the design to bars, restaurants and nightclubs in the city raised Motta's visibility and he received the Museu da Casa Brasileira's coveted Design Award.

Today, from his atelier in São Paulo's Vila Madalena neighborhood, Motta designs series for a furniture manufacturer in the south of Brazil and also maintains an artisanal furniture line with small-scale production, often using reused wood, such as the resistant *peroba rosa* taken from demolished houses and scrapyards. Motta strives to reduce the environmental impact of his designs and save as much energy as possible, avoiding the use of newly deforested wood and machinery in their production.

Born in São Paulo, 1952

1.

2.

3.

4.

5.

6.

1.
CM7 Chair, 1985

2.
São Paulo Chair, 2013

3.
Asturias Rocking Chair,
2002

4.
Rio Manso Armchair,
2008

5.
Asturias Rocking Chair,
2002

6.
Asturias Armchair, 2002

7.
Guaiuba Chair, 2005

8.
CM7 Armchair, 1985

9.
Braz Armchair, 2006

7.

8.

9.

Fernando Prado

Fernando Prado is Brazil's best-known lighting designer. His work is original, versatile and functional and his simple designs often encourage interaction from the user, offering various settings for different light intensity. 'What fascinates me most about lighting design is that not only can we design the form of the piece, but also its light, and that light has the power to change people's moods, which is very exciting', Prado says.

The designer studied industrial design in São Paulo and his first professional work was an internship at the Lumini company, which at the time specialized in corporate lighting solutions and collaborative projects with architectural firms. After a brief stint with another office, Prado returned to Lumini, where today he is Creative Director, coordinating engineers, production technicians and draftsmen and women in the products division, and was responsible for beginning their residential lighting line.

Prado's dual roles — both designer and curator of product lines — have helped contributed to the excellence of his production both from an aesthetic and technological point of view. To him, the challenge of production is using industry technology without losing artistic character. The designer has collected prizes from some of the most renowned Brazilian and international design competitions, such as the Good Design, Design Plus, the German Design Award and Museu da Casa Brasileira's design prize.

Born in São Paulo, 1971

1.
Lift Lamp

2.
Bauhaus 90 Lamp

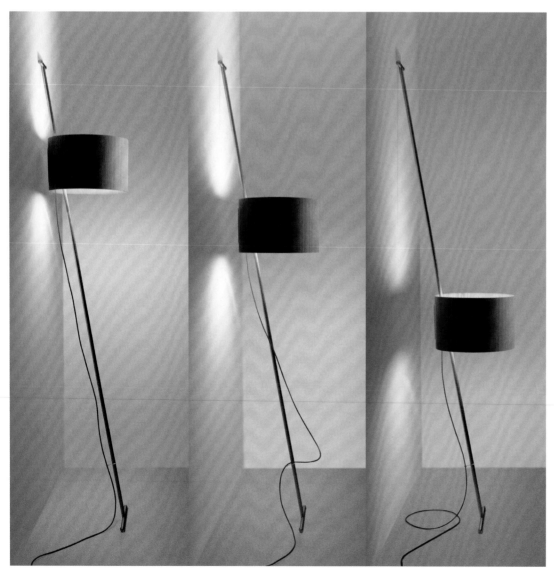

1.

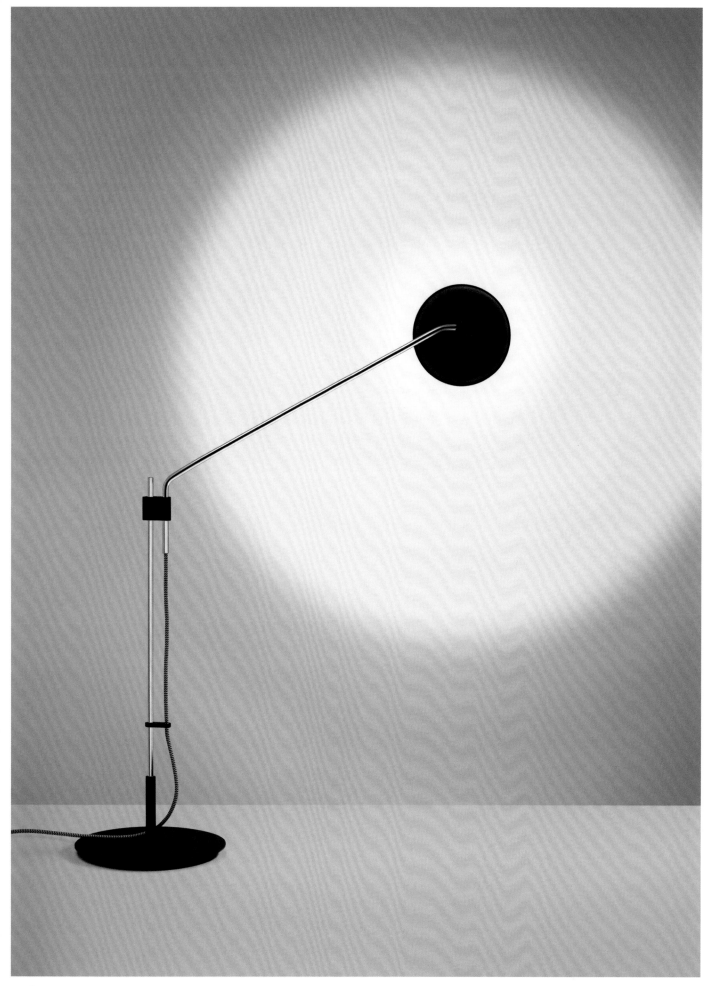

2.

3.

4.

5.

3.
Fool Lamp

4–5.
Bossa Light

6.
Luna Light

6.

Jader Almeida

Jader Almeida is one of the rising stars of Brazilian design. With great stamina and creative energy, in little more than ten years he has accumulated a notable collection of almost 150 pieces in production — all sharing an original design, technical excellence and top-quality finishes.

Almeida often says that his work strives for silent, timeless beauty: it doesn't 'shout', he says, it is not made to steal the stage. In fact, his designs follow the bare, streamlined ideal. With finesse and boldness, they reference the work of the Brazilian Modernists he admires, such as Sergio Rodrigues.

Almeida began his studies in technical design at the age of 15, and from then on became familiar with the manufacturing culture, working in the various stages of the furniture production chain. This experience was fundamental for his current professional activities — he now divides his time amongst all the stages of design, from product development and sales to working on prototypes, researching materials, distribution analysis, logistics and marketing.

Creative director of Brazilian company Sollos since 2004, Almeida has modernized the company's procedures, increased its production capacity, reworked its commercial planning and revamped the marketing campaigns of its collections. Investment in new equipment means that the furniture they produce can be much more technically complex than the majority of Brazilian production, an advantage that Almeida takes advantage of with his light, sinuous forms.

Born in Santa Catarina, 1981

1.

2.

3.

4.

1.
Mark Stool (cork)

2.
Wed Side Table

3.
Roots Wood Coffee Table

4.
Cigg Side Table

5.
Bossa Chair

6.
Easy Chair

7.
Loose Hanger

8.
Euvira Rocking Chair

5.

6.

7.

8.

Marcelo Rosenbaum

Already well known for his artisanal production and versatility, designing everything from São Paulo Fashion Week runway events, Rio Carnival VIP areas and retail spaces to furniture lines, fabrics and products, Marcelo Rosenbaum shot to fame when he appeared in the *Lar Doce Lar* (Home Sweet Home) series on Globo, Brazil's largest television channel, from 2005 to 2012.

The concept of the series was to offer disadvantaged families the chance to have their houses transformed for free. Rosenbaum was the first designer to participate in the programme. He conceived the general remodelling of the interiors, installations and facades and the purchase of equipment and utensils according to the style and desires of the residents. In seven years of the series, nearly 70 houses were remodelled and the show elevated the profile of the design profession in front of a national audience.

Today, Rosenbaum works on the social design project *A Gente Transforma* (We Transform) with two indigenous communities, one in the state of Piauí in the north, and another in the western state of Acre. A multidisciplinary group including designers invited by Rosenbaum immerses itself in the community, gets to know the local traditions, utensils and customs of the people, and through this understanding, works together on an artisanal production process.

In the project with the community from Acre, the studios of Rosenbaum, Fetiche and Nada se Leva worked with a team of nearly 80 artisans to create a collection of lamps made of beads, straw and vines based on the myths of the local indigenous people. The products are finished and commercialized by La Lampe and sold in several cities throughout Brazil.

Born in São Paulo, 1968

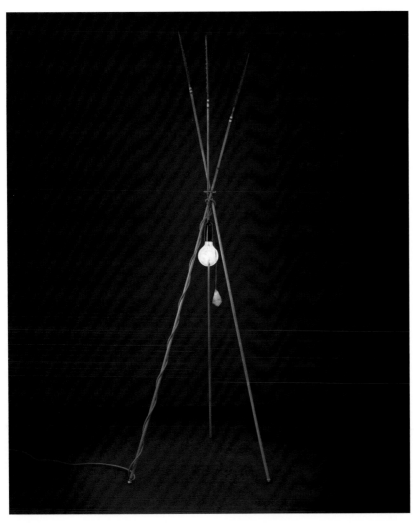

1.

1.
Puriti Lamp

2.
Shunuã Lamp

3.
Runuãrunuahu Lamp

4.
Runuakene Lamp

2.

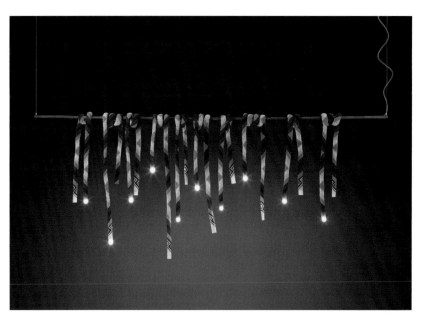

3.

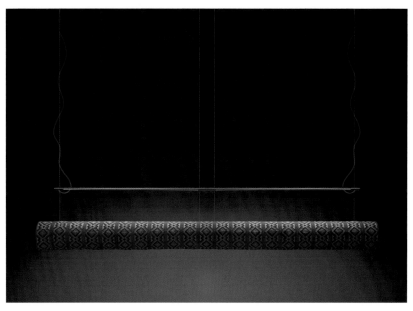

4.

5.

6.

7.

8.

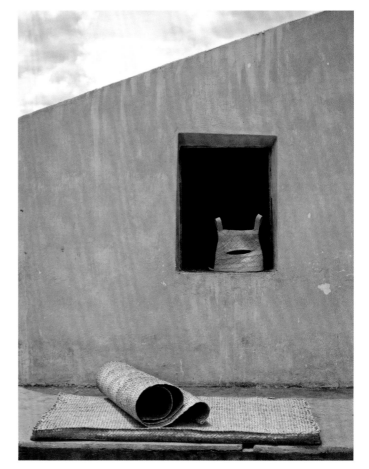

9.

10.

OVO

Luciana Martins and Gerson de Oliveira studied film and met each other at the University of São Paulo at the end of the 1980s. They founded the OVO company in 1991 and, since then, have created furniture, lamps and other objects that are recognizable for their plastic qualities, bold forms and playful nature.

OVO's projects target contemporary urban homes, and their chairs, benches, tables and lighting designs feature well-composed colour palettes and quality materials and take on a beautiful, full-bodied appearance of practicality and modularity.

With regular annual collections, the duo has recently also collaborated on a number of interior design projects for museums and exhibitions. Since the launch of their armchair *Cadê* (Where is it?), an iron structure hidden under a suspended cloth covering, OVO has accumulated some of the most important design prizes in the country, including mentions and awards from the Museu da Casa Brasileira and Brasil faz Design.

Founded in São Paulo, 1991

1.
Home Sweet Home, 2000

2.
Boiling, 2013

3.
Campo, 2007

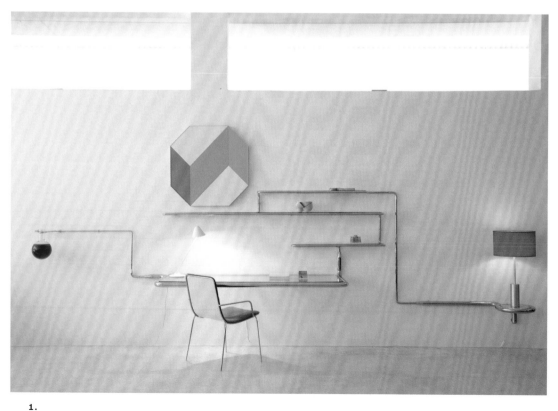

1.

2.

3.

Domingos Tótora

Born and raised in Maria da Fé, a small city in the mountainous region of Minas Gerais, Domingos Tótora moved to São Paulo for a few years to study art and design at FAAP (Armando Álvares Penteado Foudation) and USP (University of São Paulo). Now back in his hometown, he creates his unique series of vases, bowls, seats, chairs, objects and sculptures.

His pieces may appear to be constructed from wood, clay or even stone, but they are actually made from a specially-produced type of recycled cardboard. After realizing how much of the material was discarded every day by businesses and institutions around him, he realised its potential as a new raw material and developed a specific technique similar to papier mache. Tótora likes to belive that his work brings an artistic aura

to objects of everyday use. 'I never conceive a work as a piece of furniture but a sculpture that will later receive a function', he says.

His pieces are the product of a team that champions sustainability and environmentally-friendly techniques, and his studio, locatated deep in the Mantiqueira Mountains, consists of around ten local people. The curvilinear shapes of his designs are inspired by the nature that surrounds him.

His work has been the focus of exhibitions in Rio de Janeiro, Berlin, Lisbon and London and he has received a number of awards in Brazil such as the Museu da Casa Brasileira Design Prize and the Prêmio TOP XXI.

Born in Maria da Fé, 1960

1.

1.
Vereda Bench

2.
Kraft Bench

3.
Semine Chair

2.

3.

Zanini de Zanine

With a career spanning just over ten years, Zanini de Zanine became a fixture on the Brazilian design scene with his distinctive, sculptural pieces made from wood, steel and aluminium. Son of the self-taught architect and designer José Zanine Caldas, he grew up around his father's work for Móveis Artísticos Z — the manufacturer founded in the 1940s that provided furniture for many Modernist houses in Brazil, such as that of president Juscelino Kubitschek in Belo Horizonte. Today some of their most successful pieces are being reissued.

Zanine graduated in industrial design in Rio and interned with one of the greatest masters of woodwork in Brazil, the designer Sergio Rodrigues. In 2003, he started to create furniture with scraps taken from demolitions.

Two years later, he began to explore new materials such as stainless steel, aluminum, acrylic and concrete. He has claimed some of the most important design awards in Brazil and designed pieces for brands such as Tolix and Poltrona Frau. Besides his father and Sergio Rodrigues, his greatest inspirations are the sculptures of Amilcar de Castro and the furniture of Joaquim Tenreiro. To the latter, Zanine attributes the lines of his Trez armchair, produced by Cappellini.

Born in Rio de Janeiro, 1978

1.
Escoras, 2013

2.
Moeda, 2010

3.
Trez, 2013

1.

2.

3.

Campana Brothers

The Campana brothers held their first exhibition in 1989. The show presented a series of chairs titled *Desconfortável* (Uncomfortable)—sculpted out of iron, they were neither welcoming nor particularly functional, but they revealed the irreverence that would go on to characterize the duo, whose work often sits on the border between art and design.

Humberto, a lawyer by training, and his architect brother Fernando, have continued to produce pieces that are defined by textures and forms obtained through artisan methods, often using natural or industrialized materials removed from their usual context. Strands of wire, twine, strips of rubber, broken mirror, bricks and tiles, synthetic leather, pieces of wood, rattan, rag dolls and stuffed animals have all become raw materials transformed by the Campanas into chairs, lamps, sofas, benches, utensils and tables.

In the 1990s, their work gained international attention with a show at MoMA in New York. Not long after, the duo joined forces with the Italian company Edra, for the *Vermelha* (Red) chair line, an iron structure held together with thick chords, like knitting needles thrust through a ball of wool. It was a significant step for the brothers at it was the first of their projects to be manufactured outside Brazil.

More recently, the Campanas have also worked with sculpture, ceramics, installations and interiors. They were behind the design of cafés at both the Municipal Theatre of São Paulo and the Musée d'Orsay in Paris, and have work in the permanent collections of MoMA in New York, the Centre Pompidou in Paris and the Vitra Design Museum in Weil am Rhein.

Despite their extensive international agenda, they still work out of their workshop in downtown São Paulo, located amongst the cheap stores and repair shops—it is here that they research materials and techniques and build prototypes of the objects that have changed the image of Brazilian design over the last fifteen years.

Humberto: born in São Paulo, 1953
Fernando: born in Brotas, 1961

1.

1.
Vermelha Chair, 1998

2.
Alligator Chair, 2004

3.
Cipria Sofa, 2009 and
Cabana Storage Units,
2010

2.

3.

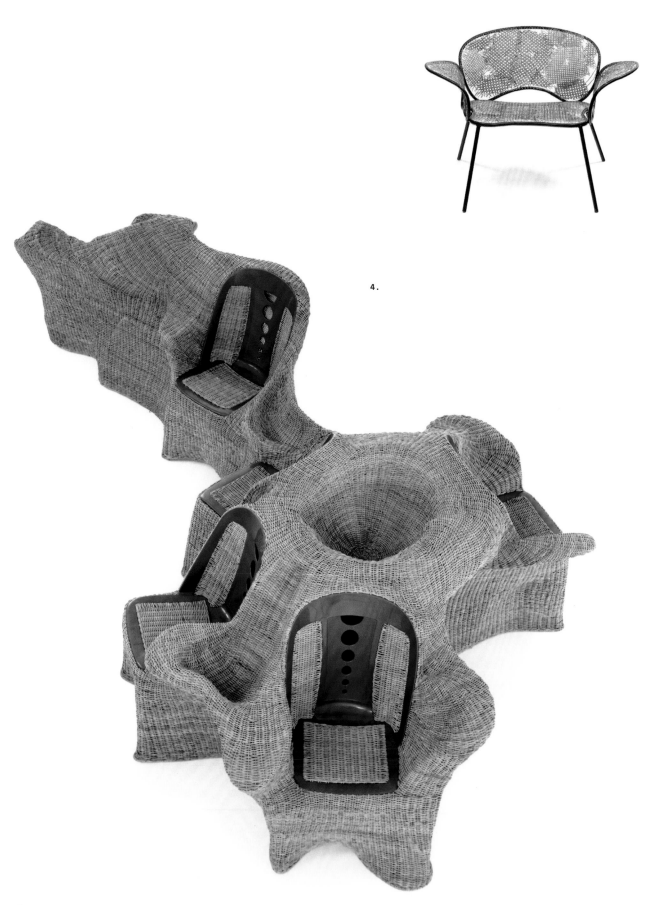

4.

5.

4.
Detonado Chair, 2013

5.
From the TransPlastic
collection, 2007

6.
Sushi Chair, 2002

7.
Boa Sofa, 2002

6.

7.

Pedro Lourenço

Adriana Barra

Antonio Bernardo

Jack Vartanian

Paula Cademartori

Barbara Casasola

Alexandre Herchcovitch

Natalie Klein

Adriana Degreas

Oskar Metsavaht

Simone Esmanhotto

fashion

In October last year, 23-year-old Pedro Lourenço—the only child of São Paulo-based designers, Gloria Coelho and Reinaldo Lourenço—presented his spring 2014 collection in Paris. Despite his youth, this was his eleventh season in the fashion capital. Today, Lourenço's clothes are generally considered the best expression of the current mood and market in Brazil. His first shows, at just twelve years old, coincided with Brazil's economic boom—in just one decade, 30 million people ascended from poverty to the middle class, and by the end of 2014, 31 million will be considered rich, earning at least R$6,000 (£1,564) a month. Lourenço has achieved a level of sophistication and excellence yet to be seen in a developing local luxury market. He stands out for his interest in technology and technique, his inventive use of leather, his patchwork of materials, his precise tailoring and his youthful yet classy urbanity. The critics are consistently impressed by this designer that they simply refer to as 'the Young Brazilian'.

It is no coincidence that his nationality is cited in a time when the 'made in …' tag gains ever more relevance. Although Brazilian by birth, designers such as Barbara Casasola with her monastic clothes, jeweller Fernando Jorge with his curvy pieces and milky stones and Milan-based Paula Cademartori with her colourful leather bags, have established a global style that is popular the world over. Even when he references the distinctive tropical style of Carmen Miranda, Lourenço's clothes are unquestionably international—his pencil skirts and trouser suits fit comfortably with the street style of New York's West Village or the Rive Gauche in Paris, but are scarcely seen on the streets of Jardins, the fashionable neighbourhood of his native São Paulo that for a long time remained the place to see and be seen. Influenced by European trends, Brazil's upper classes tend to look for their elegance on the other side of the Atlantic—Lourenço's dresses, which often sell for around R$3,000 (£776), around four times the monthly minimum wage in Brazil, are made to compete with the likes of Prada and Dolce & Gabbana. His aesthetic, which is strict and architectural with leather elements, makes more sense abroad than it does at home, where average summer temperatures regularly exceed 25°C (77°F).

Ever since the Portuguese colonization in 1500, the upper classes have been educated in the lexicon of French fashion. The fortunes made from the rubber extraction in Belém, in the northern state of Pará, made it possible for women to buy pieces by Charles Frederick Worth and send them back by ship just to be washed in Paris. Rio de Janeiro was listed alongside Brussels and Geneva as the third destination outside France to receive the Parisian *Le Petit Echo de la Mode* (a weekly magazine of trends in fashion, beauty and art de vivre in the nineteenth century) and in the 1950s, Jacques Fath, Christian Dior and Pierre Balmain were favourites for weddings and cocktail parties, as the dresses on display in the museums of Rio testify. Meanwhile social columns debated the virtues of Cristóbal Balenciaga's sac dresses with respect to the taste of traditional Brazilian husbands and their love of the hourglass figure.

In Brazil, the apparel industry dates from the 1970s. Before then, it was copies of the outfits seen on the models in European newspapers and magazines that gave the country a sense of sartorial style. Unsurprisingly for one of the world's biggest producers of cotton, denim jeans remain a best-seller. Small local factories flood the market with T-shirts and a multitude of viscose dresses. The sphere of influence has shifted from Europe to the United States, culminating in a mixture of hip hop meets South Beach Miami. Recent prosperity brought in more cars, more cell phones and more international

1.

2.

3.

4.

2—3.
Gloria Coelho, Summer
2015 collection, São
Paulo Fashion Week

4.
Reinaldo Lourenço,
Fall/Winter 2013
collection, São Paulo
Fashion Week

brands, changing the retail landscape dramatically over the last two years. Three new shopping malls — Cidade Jardim and JK Iguatemi in São Paulo and Village Mall in Rio — now offer everything from Chanel to Louis Vuitton. JK Iguatemi, which opened in 2013, includes 189 stores, 60 of which are international brands and 30 of those were completely new to the Brazilian market. Last year marked the expansion of international brands to malls in southern Curitiba and northern Recife, taking international designer labels to a completely new audience.

What seems like a crisis for the home-grown fashion industry may actually be an opportunity for creativity. As poverty is on the decline in Brazil and the number of wealthy citizens is on the rise, a second wave of consumerism is starting to take place. Standardization and price limitations are being replaced with sophisticated choices and higher standards. Mid-tier brands such as Tory Burch and Kate Spade benefited hugely from the new wave of money from people interested in paying a bit more for better quality and more originality. The fast fashion chains started investing in design. From 1979, Riachuelo was transformed from a destination for cheap clothes to Brazil's largest and most popular fast fashion chain, inviting Brazilian designers to collaborate yet still offering low prices. Present in Brazil since 1976, global giant C&A reinvented itself in 2011, launching capsule collections by Stella McCartney, Roberto Cavalli and Brazilian designers such as Alexandre Herchcovitch.

With a 20-year-strong career, Herchcovitch remains the most established name at São Paulo Fashion Week and has mastered the art of democratizing design. Rising from the underground scene in São Paulo, he made a name for himself by defying bourgeoisie conventions and his brand was bought by a local conglomerate in 2008. Today, Herchcovitch stands out as one of the only creative forces capable of selling his name on products from eyewear to Melissa Jelly Shoes, and his jeans line, presented at Fashion Rio, opened up Brazilian design to include the kind of clothes Brazilians love to wear.

Combined with a developing local market, the interest and level of demand of international buyers may be the final push that the Brazilian fashion scene needs to develop its way to maturity. International market heavy-weights have started coming to the country looking for fashion voices. At the end of 2013, two major virtual movements started taking place: buyers of the Florence-based luxury online store, Luisaviaroma came to São Paulo to select brands, and London-based Farfetch, who already operate in Brazil, decided to make local brands available to international consumers. The Japanese department store Isetan also came shopping. In 2013, Le Bon Marché organised *Le Brésil Rive Gauche*, a three-month season of curated local products. The initiative drew the attention of the French retail chain Monoprix, who researched ways to attract a crowd seduced by the Brazilian spirit, producing exclusive yet accessible products in Brazil. Until recently Brazil was better known for exporting fashion commodities designed by foreigners — for example, Oscar de la Renta shoes have long been made in the factories in the south of the country — but things are changing. São Paulo-based shoe designer Alexandre Birman, who comes from a lineage of shoemakers and sells his locally-produced pairs to the likes of Bergdorf Goodman, is just one of the home-grown talents producing in Brazil and selling abroad.

The 'wow' factor fashion experts are looking for in Brazilian design may lie in a designer's ability to turn their back on the prevailing trend for transatlantic elegance and take their inspiration from the rich cultural heritage around them. Indeed, when impresario Paulo Borges organized São Paulo Fashion Week, his major quest was to define Brazilian fashion.

Although exotic prints of colourful macaws, toucans and tropical fruit are still highly appealing, they form just a small part of Brazil's visual culture. Véronique Nichanian, head of menswear at Hermès, has said in the past how impressed she is with the ability of Brazilians to mix colours and prints and to reject rigid protocol. The 'wow' factor expected from Brazilian fashion will never rise artificially, with designers working away from the streets, looking to please colonial tastes, and it may take time to come, but there's a genuine chance it will happen in the next few years. And leading the way will most likely be Osklen, a brand headed by Oskar Metsavaht that sells the lifestyle of Ipanema beach in Rio to an international audience. *Cariocas*, the city's residents, are arguably the Brazilian equivalent of Parisiens, reflecting their art de vivre in their clothing.

As design intelligence approaches the streets, connecting creativity with local necessities, Brazilians may start innovating and researching materials, working closely with the industry. One still sees fragile leather-soled shoes sold in northern Brazil, where it rains religiously, or impossibly thick suits for men to wear on hot São Paulo summer days. The new wave of consumers will realize sooner or later that a suit made of extra-thin linen is more appropriate than polyamide for the heat and that rubber will resist, with far more elegance, a tropical tempest. However, there is a long way to go, be it in fibres or craftsmanship, and an entire country to explore. Richness is the motor of style and Brazil is rich enough, especially in inspiration, to find its own voice in the international fashion scene.

5.
Lenny Niemeyer, Summer
2012 collection, Rio
Fashion Week

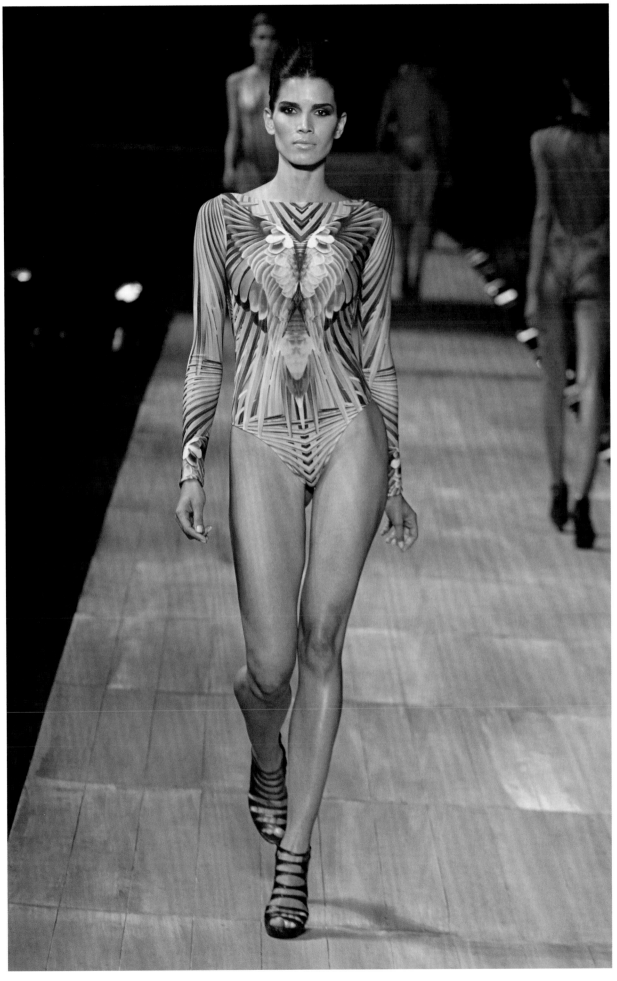

5.

Pedro Lourenço

Pedro Lourenço, the youngest and arguably the most respected of Brazil's international fashion designers, is the only child of fashion duo Gloria Coelho and Reinaldo Lourenço, who reigned the São Paulo design scene in the 1990s and continue to release collections today. He has clearly inherited his parents' taste for couture, eye for tailoring and their sharp, architectural style, whilst adding his own passion for working with cutting-edge technology and leather.

Lourenço started young: his formative years were spent learning design and pattern techniques at his parents' studios. He showed his first collection at just seven years old and took over Carlota Joakina, his mother's second label, at twelve. In 2005, he presented his own collection at São Paulo Fashion week, and five years later saw the debut of his first ready-to-wear collection at Paris Fashion Week, sealing his reputation as one

of fashion's most talented young creatives. Lourenço developed a range of sharp, futuristic dresses, coats and trousers made from panels of leather, plastic and double-faced wool felt. Plastic strips sewn into beaded, venetian blind-like grids added extra dimension to many of the pieces.

Receiving instant critical acclaim for his contemporary design aesthetic and strong creative identity, Lourenço's collection proved a hit with industry insiders and drew early comparisons to Nicholas Ghesquière for his clean, minimalist style. He has collaborated with Brazilian shoe designer Melissa on a capsule shoe collection in 2012, and an accessories range for Swarovski, and cites his main inspirations as Diana the huntress and Oscar Niemeyer.

Born in São Paulo, 1990

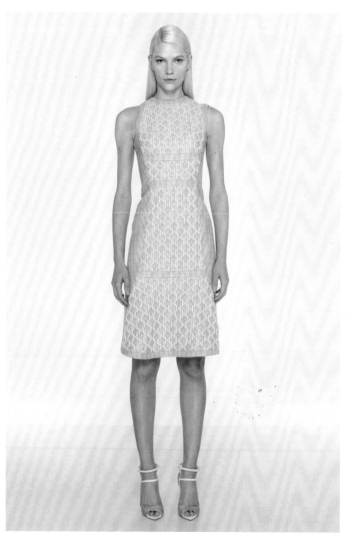

1.

2.

1–2.
Cruise/Resort
collection 2012

3.
Fall/Winter
collection 2014

4–7.
Fall/Winter
collection 2013

3.

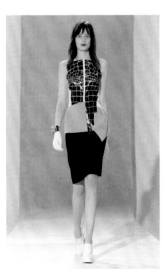

4.

5.

6.

7.

8.

9.

10.

11.

8–11.
Spring/Summer
collection 2014

12.
Spring/Summer
collection 2014

12.

Adriana Barra

Adriana Barra has made a name for herself out of vibrant, psychedelic floral prints, applying them to everything from shirts and skirts, to wallpapers and parasols. She began her career in fashion in the mid-2000s by adapting the simple traditional styles and motifs of northern Brazil for an everyday wardrobe: the chintzy prints more commonly used on tablecloths thus became long colorful cotton dresses to be worn with flowers in the hair and the white Renascença-lace, introduced to Brazil by nuns in the sixteenth century and nowadays mainly used for sheets and curtains, was transformed into blouses.

Although at the start of her career Barra paid more attention to the patterns of her sophisticated prints than the cut and design of her outfits, her more recent collections are increasingly elegant. Her shirts and trousers have became instant hits with the hip crowd that travel regularly between the metropolis of São Paulo and the beaches of Rio, and Barra's collection was one of the biggest successes in Le Brésil au Bon Marché, a three-month season of Brazilian products at the department store in Paris.

Barra's style cashes in on the popularity of bohemian-chic and there is something distinctly Brazilian about her fashion line, which cleverly injects a laid-back tropical elegance into urban clothes and luxury fabrics.

Born in Londrina, 1974

1.

2.

1–2.
Adriana Barra prints

3.
Wicca collection,
Winter 2014

4.
Beach umbrella
designs, 2014

5.
High Summer
collection 2014

3.

4.

5.

6–7.
Summer collection 2013

8.
Winter collection 2013

9–11.
Summer collection 2013

6.

7.

8.

9.

10.

11.

Antonio Bernardo

Jeweller Antonio Bernardo has built his thirty-year career around his obsession with giving form to gold — and, more recently, silver. His pieces share something in common with the architecture of Oscar Niemeyer and the furniture of Sergio Rodrigues, with their curves and folds giving an unexpected weightlessness to a solid material, something the Modernist masters achieved with concrete and wood.

Being the son of a store owner who imported and sold instruments to goldsmiths and watchmakers in the centre of Rio de Janeiro, Bernardo came into contact with the goldsmith trade through his father, and his first jewellery in the 1970s was made using his equipment. In 1968 he travelled to Lausanne, Switzerland, to study at CFH (Centre International de Formation de L'Industrie Horlogère Suisse), and intern at watch making companies Ebauches and Leschot. Back in Brazil, he enrolled on an engineering course in Rio de Janeiro, but never completed it, deciding instead to dedicate his time to researching goldsmith techniques and teaching himself the art of jewellery making.

Bernardo opened his first shop in 1981, and in 2000, launched a flagship store in Ipanema, along with the Antonio Bernardo Gallery, which holds contemporary art exhibitions. Today, he has shops all over Brazil and is represented in stores across the USA, Europe and Asia.

Born in Rio de Janeiro, 1947

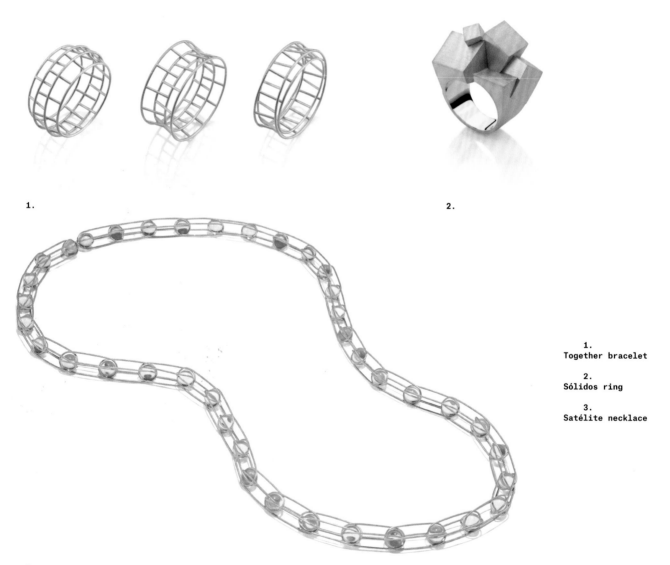

1.

2.

1.
Together bracelet

2.
Sólidos ring

3.
Satélite necklace

3.

Jack Vartanian

Jack Vartanian has been creating fine jewellery collections infused with a unique blend of tradition, sophistication and avant-garde design since 1999. The son of a Lebanese gemstone wholesaler who moved to São Paulo, Vartanian followed his father around the world on trips to Germany, India, Japan and Thailand. He studied economics whilst working full-time for his father's business, but soon became frustrated with the quality of jewellery design in Brazil, deciding he could become a successful designer himself.

Today, Vartanian launches new collections with surprising regularity, using materials such as gold, rhodium, black diamonds, emeralds and sapphires, and mixing old-world glamour with a modern aesthetic to create jewellery inspired by his native Brazil. 'I think my design reflects Brazil's colours, sex appeal, and its cheerful lifestyle. Just think of *bossa nova*, "*The Girl From Ipanema*," the carioca groove... Brazilian gemstones are very inspiring', he says.

His retail locations include stores in São Paulo and Rio de Janeiro, as well as a flagship boutique on Madison Avenue, in New York City. His collections can also be seen in the famed American department store Barney's, and have been worn by numerous celebrities including Jessica Alba, Kate Beckinsale and Zoe Saldana.

Born in Beirut, 1972

1.

2.

1.
Gala Drop ring

2.
Pedro Lourenço ring

3.
Teardrop ring

4.
Gala Punk earrings with emeralds and baguette diamonds

3.

4.

Paula Cademartori

Paula Cademartori moved to Italy in 2005, after graduating in industrial design. Once in Milan, she continued her education, gaining a Master's degree (magna cum laude) in Fashion Accessories from the Istituto Marangoni, and a 'Young Fashion Manager' certificate from Bocconi University's School of Business.

She started her career as Junior Accessories Designer for the Versace fashion house, where she was responsible for the design of the leather goods for the women's Couture and Prêt-à-Porter collections. In September 2009, she was selected for the *Vogue Talents* project and she was included in *Vogue Italia*'s list of Emerging Designers, thanks to her refined footwear collection for Spring/Summer 2010.

In 2010, Cademartori launched her own brand, with the release of its first Spring/Summer handbag collection at Milan Fashion Week in 2011. With a keen eye for structure and detail, she has infused youthful attitude into the status bag with graphic embellishments, handcrafted constructions and playful hues. She works with special leathers such as crocodile, lizard and python to produce her colourful bags, which are jewel-like on the outside, yet practical on the inside. Cademartori designs everything herself and supervises the Milan-based production. Her bags are now sold worldwide, from China to Saudi Arabia, and from the USA to Japan.

Born in Porto Alegre, 1983

1.

1.
Tatiana, Spring/Summer
2013

2.
Alice, Pre-Spring/
Summer 2014

3.
Anna, Pre-Spring/
Summer 2014

4.
Kate, Pre-Spring/
Summer 2014

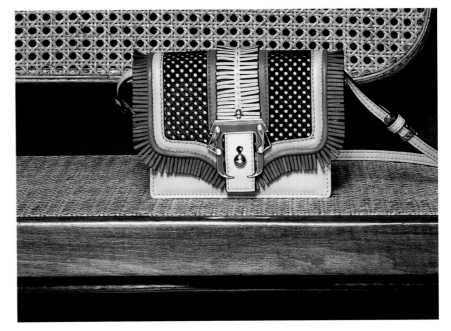

2.

3.

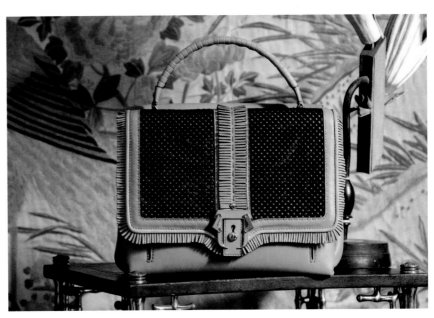

4.

Barbara Casasola

UK-based Barbara Casasola, who was raised in the far-south of Brazil, graduated in fashion design from London's Central Saint Martins before attending the Istituto Marangoni in Milan. On completion of her studies, she was hired by Roberto Cavalli in Florence, where she was first assistant designer for womenswear for over two years. She subsequently moved to Paris in January 2010 to work alongside Gabriele Greiss (former Creative Director at Sonia Rykiel) on assignments for Lanvin and See by Chloe, before launching her own brand in 2012.

Her debut collection, presented at London Fashion Week in 2013, dispelled the clichéd image of Brazilian carnival, yet still drew on uniquely Brazilian themes and styles. Casasola is continually inspired by her native country, citing three key elements in her work: the clean lines of its rich, Modernist tradition, the Baroque aesthetic of its noble heritage and the mystery of its natural beauty.

Her collections are characterized by contrasts—rich natural fabrics are often set against modern technical fibres, solid panels next to transparent sections and matte finishes alongside glossy elements. Today, Casasola designs from her studio in London and her collections are sold worldwide in over twenty countries.

Born in Porto Alegre, 1984

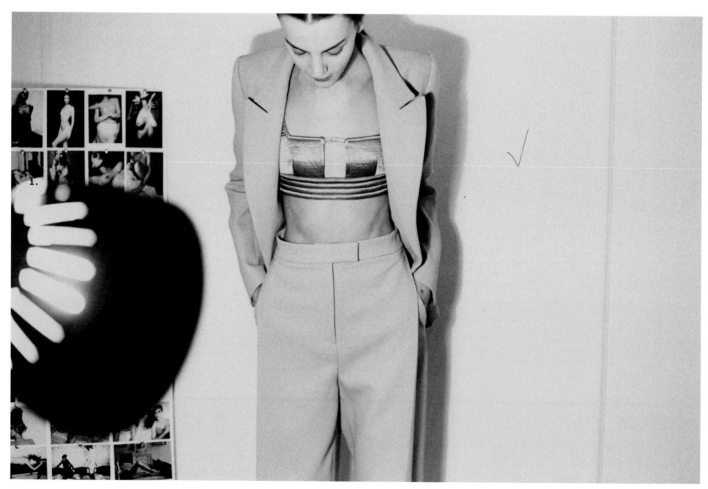

1.

4.

2.

3.

5.

1–2.
Fall/Winter
collection 2014

3.
Pre-Fall collection,
2014

4–5.
Fall/Winter
collection 2014

6.

6.
Spring/Summer
collection 2014

7–8.
Fall/Winter
collection 2014

9.
Spring/Summer
collection 2014

7.

8.

9.

Alexandre Herchcovitch

Alexandre Herchcovitch has been one of the strongest names in Brazilian fashion since the 1990s. Best known for his avant-garde design aesthetic, trademark skull motifs, use of moulded rubber and subversive portrayals of religious iconography, Herchcovitch launched his eponymous brand in 1994 and quickly became one of the most exciting names to present at the São Paulo Fashion Week.

He learnt how to sew from his mother at just ten years old, and soon began to sell his creations to family and friends. As a teenager he frequented São Paulo's alternative nightclubs whilst studying at a religious zionist Orthodox Jewish school. These conflicting ideologies continue to have a strong influence on the designer's work.

His designs have since been seen on the runways of New York, Paris, London and São Paulo Fashion Weeks, with his greatest hits including a dress made from Tyvek and a new take on the tuxedo. Herchcovitch opened his first store in Tokyo where, along with his native Brazil, he is exceptionally popular, and his designs are sold in the USA, Canada, England, France, Spain and Australia.

Born in São Paulo, 1971

1.

2.

1–2.
Fall/Winter
collection 2014

3–5.
Spring/Summer
collection 2014

3.

4.

5.

Natalie Klein

Natalie Klein, an architecture graduate from the FAAP University in São Paulo, launched luxury multi-brand boutique NK Store in 1997 at the age of 21. The store's meticulously curated selection of products from designers such as Chloé and Blumarine made the most of the fact that Brazil had recently opened the market to imported goods, and established a name for quality and pared-back chic.

The launch of Klein's two in-house labels — the exclusive NK collection released shortly after the 1997 store launch and the diffusion line Talie NK in 1999 — met with rave reviews, garnering an elite Brazilian following for the labels' two seasonal collections. Klein says that back in 1997, it was a new idea in Brazil to offer what she calls 'cool luxury', meaning non-ostentatious fashion. Her store started a process of instruction, teaching clients about the modern fashion culture and encouraging them to try new experiences focusing on 'citizens of the world, who travel and want more sophisticated clothes'. The formula has proven so successful that Klein's pieces are now available all over Brazil: Talie NK, her more affordable line, is sold at more than sixty different stores and she continues to sell international brands in her two boutiques in São Paulo and Rio de Janeiro.

Born in São Paulo, 1971

1–2.
Fall/Winter
collection 2014

1.

2.

Adriana Degreas

Brazil is known for creating some of the most glamorous swimwear in the world, and Adriana Degreas is one of the most respected names in Brazil's competitive luxury beachwear industry. Introduced to the business by her husband, whose family has been producing swimming suits and bikinis for more than 60 years, Degreas learned through him both the skills of production and important lessons in style, and after ten years she launched her eponymous brand in 2004.

Her designs are destined for the private pools and cocktail parties of Brazil's jet-set crowd, inspired by the classic images of American photographer Slim Aarons and the style of early 1960s swimming suits — the era of caftans, kimonos, turbans, drapery and lamé.

Degreas's pieces are the epitome of iconic Brazilian beachwear: elegant, sensual and impeccably made. Her prints interpret Brazilian heritage through graphic and figurative designs featuring everything from flowers and palm trees to seahorses and fish multiplied in mesmerizing Escheresque forms. With stores throughout the world, she remains a Brazilian icon and trendsetter. She has also extended her collection to the winter season, producing fur coats, knitwear and other warmer garments.

Born in São Paulo, 1971

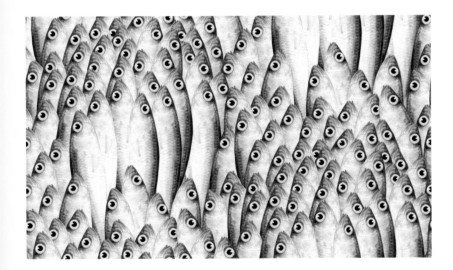

1.

1–4.
Adriana Degreas
swimwear prints,
2013–14

2.

3.

4.

Oskar Metsavaht

The fashion brand Osklen was born in 1989 with particularly surreal origins: on returning from a mountain climbing trip in Europe, Oskar Metsavaht, a surf and snowboard enthusiast, decided to open a store to sell his own line of snow wear in Búzios, the Brazilian coastal resort immortalized by Brigitte Bardot in the 1960s. Although a beach town with an average temperature of 27°C (80°F) might seem an odd place to launch a winter sports range, Metsavaht understood that the clientele who spent their summers in Búzios could well use the opportunity to buy gear for their winter trips to the USA or Europe. He was not only right, but his instinct was so correct he now figures in the Forbes list of up and coming billionaires.

Metsavaht made his career in Rio de Janeiro and today his Osklen brand sells the image and lifestyle of one of the world's most famous beaches — Ipanema. His cool, casual fashion is increasingly popular and often makes the most of eco-friendly fabrics and materials. Although the brand began with a focus on sportswear, after ten years Metsavaht refocused the brand on the luxury segment.

In 2011, Osklen received the title of 'emerging luxury brand of the year' in London, and he was pronounced by Fast Company Magazine as the 'fourth most innovative person in Brazil and one of the 100 most creative people in the business world'. Metsavaht shows his collections at New York Fashion Week and São Paulo Fashion Week.

Born in Caxias do Sul, 1961

1.

2.

1.
Fall/Winter
collection 2013

2.
Fall/Winter
collection 2012

3.
Spring/Summer
collection 2014

3.

4.

5.

6.

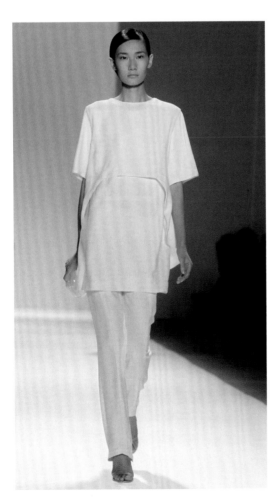

4.
Fall/Winter
collection 2014

5.
Spring/Summer
collection 2013

6.
Spring/Summer
collection 2015

7–8.
Spring/Summer
collection 2014

7.

8.

Cláudio Assis

José Padilha

Fernando Meirelles

Heitor Dhalia

Laís Bodanzky

Jorge Furtado

Kleber Mendonça Filho

Rodrigo Teixeira

Karim Aïnouz

Daniel Filho

Rodrigo Fonseca

film

Many would argue that Brazilian cinema is enjoying one of its finest moments. In fact, the national cinematographic market hasn't witnessed such a creative and productive phase since the *Cinema Novo* period, a movement that arose at the start of the 1960s. According to numbers from the Agência Nacional do Cinema (ANCINE, or National Film Agency), the federal agency in charge of cinematographic activity in Brazil, in 2013 more than 120 Brazilian productions were released, resulting in the sale of over 26 million box office tickets. It was the first time in nearly thirty-five years that the country registered nine blockbusters, among them *Minha Mãe é uma Peça* (My Mom is a Character), by André Pellenz, *O Concurso* (The Contest), by Pedro Vasconcelos and *Meu Passado me Condena*, by Júlia Rezende—all first-time directors.

The good news is that these figures consolidate a trend that has been emerging over the past five years. Since 2009, at least 100 national films have entered the market every year. Yet, like the rest of the world, the industry has seen its fair share of crises: street cinemas are becoming a thing of the past and large cinema companies rely heavily on popcorn sales to stay solvent as technological advances mean more people are staying at home to watch films.

The truth is that, after years of neglecting scripts and production, Brazil's national film industry finally realized the necessity of sticking to the proven formulas that have driven the entertainment industry elsewhere. Consequently, Brazilian filmography has grown like never before, with more educational courses appearing across all areas of the industry—including technical courses. Video producers, once focused on advertising, have begun targeting the big screen, and since 2001, there have been numerous original productions across a wide variety of genres. Indeed, during this period, associated with the terms '*retomada*' and '*pós-retomada*' (literally, resumption and post-resumption), Brazilian films have also garnered international attention, with comedies, musical biographies and thrillers about urban violence in the country's *favelas*. These works have revitalized Brazil's cinematographic scene. It is no coincidence that, according to ANCINE, some 230 Brazilian directors have emerged in the last ten years.

Brazilian cinema was born of modest origin in 1897, beginning with simple films that registered the exuberance of national landscapes. *Vista da Baía de Guanabara*, made by an Italian dramatist, would classify as the first film made in Brazil, but up until the 1940s, very few films were produced in the country. Hoping to give Brazilians the same technical quality and production offered by the best cinemas in the world, at the close of the 1940s a group of São Paulo bankers united with the engineer Franco Zampari to create the production company Vera Cruz. The model used to create the company was imported from Hollywood: European-made machines, large studios, a fixed cast and directors. The team included directors who had studied outside the country, such as Alberto Cavalcanti, and foreigners like Tom Payne, Luciano Salce and British photographer Chick Fowle. In five years, eighteen films were shown (of twenty-two produced). But the distribution of the reels was always problematic, and in the mid 1950s the company was declared bankrupt.

Contrary to the big studios, at the end of the 1950s, a movement by directors to rescue the film industry emerged in Rio de Janeiro. Known as *Cinema Novo* and strongly influenced by Italian Neorealism, its peak would arrive in 1963, with the release of three films: *Os Fuzis* (The Guns), by Ruy Guerra, *Deus e o Diabo na Terra do Sol* (Black God, White Devil) by Glauber Rocha and *Vidas Secas* (Barren Lives), by Nelson Pereira dos Santos. The Bahian director Glauber Rocha was the movement's protagonist, and he was responsible for the philosophy 'an idea in the head and a camera in the hands' that guid-

1.
Central do Brasil
(Central Station),
Walter Salles, 1998

2.
Linha de Passe, Walter
Salles, 2008

3.
Terra Estrangeira
(Foreign Land), Walter
Salles, 1996

1.

3.

2.

ed the way he and his colleagues made their films. Though not associated with this movement, but also in Rio de Janeiro, another important name in Brazilian drama emerged: Domingos de Oliveira. Oliveira produced the witty, verbal comedy with a strong Rio accent, *Todas as Mulheres do Mundo* (All the Women in the World).

The military coup in 1964 slowed the pace of production in the country. The restrictions imposed by the regime were outlined in the Institutional Act Number 5, published in December of 1968, which detailed the censorship of songs, films and the news that could be printed in newspapers, magazines and exhibited on TV channels. However, it was during the 1980s that Brazilian cinema really began to decline. With the economic crisis, the costs of production increased dramatically and the price of tickets kept most people out of theatres.

It was during the government of Fernando Collor de Mello that Brazilian cinema suffered its last great loss. In 1990, coinciding with the banking crisis that provoked the confiscation of all Brazilians' savings accounts, Embrafilme, Concine and the Cinema Brasileiro Foundation — organizations that financed film-making — all closed their doors for the last time, and the number of films produced dropped dramatically.

The *retomada*, or resumption, of Brazilian cinema, which critics tend to associate with the film *Carlota Joaquina, Princess Of Brazil*, by Carla Camurati, in 1995, was made possible by the founding of ANCINE and the arrival of the multiplex cinema — installed in shopping centres in all the major Brazilian cities. *Central do Brasil* (Central Station), by Walter Salles, Jr., released in 1998 and awarded a Golden Bear at the Berlin International Film Festival, along with several other prizes, was another great success. It even made it to the Oscars: Walter Salles, Jr. was nominated for Best Director and Fernanda Montenegro, the leading lady of national drama, was nominated for Best Actress.

The greatest example of the *retomada* is undoubtedly *Cidade de Deus* (City of God), by Fernando Meirelles. Released in 2002, the film has become one of the biggest cultural phenomena to emerge from Brazil and was the first to take the debate over the position of the *favela* within Brazil's political landscape to the big screen. Subsequently, a new generation of unknown performers rose to stardom, starting the trend of using non-actors in big films and delineating a sub-genre that identified with, and gave voice to, the disenfranchised: the *favela* movie. The film received four Oscar nominations — for directing, cinematography, adapted screenplay and editing — and although it didn't win any statues in Hollywood, it collected prizes both within Brazil and abroad, including two Baftas, for Best Foreign Film and Best Editing.

In 2003, there were more positive signs of the market picking up: films produced in Brazil — with special attention to hits such as *Carandiru* by Hector Babenco, *Lisbela e o Prisioneiro* by Guel Arraes and *Os Normais* (The Normal Ones) by José Alvarenga — accounted for twenty-two per cent of the market share. It was the healthiest year for Brazilian cinema since 1978 and the most expressive of the *retomada*. The aforementioned three films couldn't be more different to one another: *Carandiru* is set in the biggest and most overcrowded jail in the city of São Paulo, describing the days before a famous confrontation between the inmates and the police that left more than one hundred prisoners dead; *Lisbela* is a fairytale from the northeast of Brazil and tells the story of Lisbela, a romantic girl that falls in love with a truck driver, Leleu, while *Os Normais* is a film based on a comic sitcom from Brazil's biggest TV channel, Globo, and revolves around a couple that is about to be married.

4.
Heitor Dhalia on the set of Serra Pelada (Bald Mountain), 2013

5.
Jose Padilha filming RoboCop, 2013

6.
Kleber Mendonça Filho on the set of O Som ao Redor (Neighboring Sounds), 2012

7.
Laís Bodansky filming A Guerra dos Paulistas, 2002

8.
Fernando Meirelles on the set of Blindness, 2007

9.
Karim Aïnouz, 2012

10.
Fernando Meirelles on the set of 360, 2011

11.
Heitor Dhalia on the set of Serra Pelada (Bald Mountain), 2013

4.

5.

6.

7.

8.

9.

10.

11.

The fact that all three were home-grown success stories proved to the inner market that it was profitable to invest in the national film industry.

It was in this context that *Tropa de Elite 2* (Elite Squad: The Enemy Within), by José Padilha, established itself as the historic record holder for box office sales, with 11.2 million tickets sold. The queues outside the cinema doors were an indication of the consolidation of the market and the success of the director, which had begun with the first *Tropa de Elite* (Elite Squad) three years earlier, and followed with the successful remake of *RoboCop* in 2014. The first in the series, *Tropa de Elite*, from 2007, drew attention to another problem faced by the Brazilian film industry: piracy. And even though there have been a number of attempts to reduce the practice, none of them have been successful. In fact, it is estimated that more than 10 million pirated DVD versions of *Tropa de Elite* have made their way onto the street.

In the last few years, a new rank of directors has emerged as part of a movement known as *Novíssimo Cinema Brasileiro* (Very New Brazilian Cinema) after the award granted to *Estrada para Ythaca* (Road to Ythaca) (2010), made by the collective Alumbramento, at the Mostra de Cinema de Tiradentes (Tiradentes Film Festival). The term *Novíssimo* (an expression coined at a Rio de Janeiro festival in 2009 organized by Lis Kogan and Eduardo Valente) refers to the school of Brazilian directors whose films, which are extremely low-budget for market standards (less than R$100,000 [£27,000]), are more concerned with script integrity than with box office performance.

Cannes Film Festival welcomed two partnerships that were key to the *Novíssimo* concept. In 2010, Marina Meliande and Felipe Bragança screened their *A Alegria* (The Joy), a kind of inverse superhero movie in the Directors' Fortnight, and the next year, the *Un Certain Regard* section of the awards opened with *Trabalhar Cansa* (Hard Labour), by Marco Dutra and Juliana Rojas, an essay on class struggle in a post-Marxist political context, shot with references to psychological thrillers *à la* Roman Polanski. Another important name associated with the *Novíssimo* concept is cinematographer Ivo Lopes Araújo, from Ceará, celebrated for his work on *Linz — Onde Todos os Acidentes Acontecem*, directed by Alexandre Veras. Seen today as the go-to director of photography amongst the younger generation of film-makers, he was responsible for the transgressive outlook of *O Homem das Multidões*, (The Man of the Crowd), which was based on an Edgar Allan Poe text, directed by Cao Guimarães and Marcelo Gomes and shot in 3×3 format.

In the midst of this renewal (and its controversies), there was a boom in video art production, as well as experiments that blurred the borders between documentary, fiction and the visual arts, particularly coming out of Minas Gerais. Hailing from that state, Cao Guimarães has established himself as one of the most relevant Brazilian directors at international festivals, including the Venice Film Festival, with experiments such as *Andarilho* (Drifter) (2006) and *A Alma do Osso* (2004). He also made *Acidente* (2005), a formal documentary based on the names of Minas Gerais towns.

Minas Gerais is just one of the centres of so-called off-circuit cinema (that is, executed outside of the more obvious metropolises, such as Rio de Janeiro and São Paulo) to experience a boom in the past ten years. Santa Catarina, for example, had minimal national influence until 2011, when Cíntia Domit Bittar's *Qual Queijo Você Quer?* (What Cheese do you Want?) was widely applauded at festivals and Zeca Nunes Pires' *A Antropóloga* (The Anthropologist) was released, putting the state on the audiovisual map. The same happened in 2012, when Sérgio Andrade's *A Floresta de Jonathas* (Jonathas' Forest) was partly produced in Manaus.

Cinemas in Brazil took a long time to grant documentaries the same treatment traditionally reserved for fiction. The Brazilian film industry was not convinced of the potential popularity of documentaries, even after witnessing director and historian Silvio Tendler turn them into box office champions in the 1980s with features such as *Os Anos JK — Uma Trajetória Política* (The JK Years: A Political Trajectory) (1980), *O Mundo Mágico dos Trapalhões* (1981) and *Jango* (1984). For decades, documentaries were relegated to the background due to the assumption that few audiences would pay to see depictions of reality. The exception, during the *retomada*, was *Todos os Corações do Mundo* (Two Billion Hearts), directed by Murilo Salles and released in 1995, with around 200,000 tickets sold. But it was regarded as an exception because it was the official World Cup movie in a year in which Brazil won the title for the fifth time in its history. However, it was during these early years of the *retomada* that Eduardo Coutinho, a director who gained international prestige in the 1980s with his cult movie *Cabra Marcado para Morrer* (Twenty Years Later), returned to the screen with a modest production that mapped the different ways in which Brazilians express their religious faith. The film was called *Santo Forte*, the year was 1999, and with it, Coutinho became one of the most prestigious documentary film-makers in the country.

Simultaneously, Marcelo Masagão surprised the public with a collage of archive images called *Nós que Aqui Estamos por Vós Esperamos*. Both this and Coutinho's film conquered critics and the public alike and made cinemas realize that the audience for documentaries was larger than they had imagined. Successful movies such as Coutinho's *Edifício Master* (2002) and João Moreira Salles's *Nelson Freire* (2003) changed the outlook of the market, which, in 2005, witnessed Miguel Faria Jr.'s *Vinícius* become the most successful documentary box office performance of the last twenty years, with 271,000 tickets sold. Today, there is no format or genre in the country that produces more films than the documentary industry. About ninety documentaries have been produced every year since 2009. The angle and the subject vary hugely, but one subgenre stands out: the musical documentary. Ranging from the intimate *Paulinho da Viola — Meu Tempo é Hoje*, directed by Izabel Jaguaribe and Zuenir Ventura, to the heavy rock of *Titãs — A Vida Parece uma Festa*, by Branco Mello and Oscar Rodrigues Alves, musical documentaries are a huge market in Brazil.

So what does the future hold? The rising number of productions has not been reflected by a similar rise in the number of cinema screens, which in 2013 was limited to around 2,700, so the struggle for visibility is intense. But, if on the one hand, this illustrates discrepancies in the country's cultural 'agrarian reform', on the other hand it highlights the growing interest of the public, who reacts to the national supply with respect and affection when it is able to access it. In the past few years, only comedies with a budget of over R$5 million (£1.3 million) — such as Bruno Barretto's *Crô* (2013) and Felipe Joffily's *E Aí, Comeu?* — have been able to secure large-scale releases. But the variety of Brazilians' tastes shows us that there are avid consumers for every kind of movie. This has been Brazil's biggest victory, film-wise.

Cláudio Assis

Pernambuco-born director Cláudio Assis became re-nowned in Brazil for his graphic depictions of sex and domestic abuse. He has directed eight films, both shorts and feature-length: *Amarelo Manga* (Mango Yellow), released in 2002 and the first feature-length movie of his career, is an extended version of the short *Texas Hotel* (1999), in which he established a connection with the combative tradition of directors such as Pier Paolo Pasolini and Marco Ferreri. The film garnered him the highest award of the Brasília Festival and the International Confederation of Art Cinemas prize in Berlin in 2002. His intention was to bring together a troupe of different characters from Recife's working class, marked by their inability to deal with love and pleasure—a recurring theme in Assis's work.

In 2007, he won the Tiger Award at the Rotterdam Film Festival for *Baixio das Bestas* (Bog of Beasts). In this, his second feature-length movie, Assis addressed *maracatu*, a typical dance of the state of Pernambuco, side-by-side with a discussion of the sexual exploitation of minors. His third movie, *Febre de Rato* (Rat Fever), was elected best film of the Paulínia Film Festival in 2011 and received critical acclaim for its black and white photography and the treatment of a marginal poet's life.

Born in Caruaru, 1959

1.

2.

1–3.
Febre do Rato
(Rat Fever), 2011

3.

José Padilha

José Padilha currently holds the Brazilian record for largest cinema audience in the past forty years—box office sales for *Tropa de Elite 2: O Inimigo Agora é Outro* (Elite Squad: The Enemy Within) (2010) reached 11 million—an impressive feat considering this was achieved without the support of multinational studios and distributors. It was the greatest commercial success in Brazil since the 1970s.

Three years earlier, the first film in the series, *Tropa de Elite* (Elite Squad), whose protagonist is played by Wagner Moura, one of the country's top actors, had fallen victim to the piracy networks after a premature copy was leaked on to the web. According to estimates by the Rio de Janeiro Military and Civil Police, around 10 million pirate DVDs of the film were sold, however, Padilha's disappointment at the consequent dip in box office sales was offset slightly when he received a Golden Bear for the film at the Berlin Film Festival.

The series, based on the real lives of the BOPE, the Special Police Operations Battalion of Rio de Janeiro, was inspired by previous documentaries by Padilha about public safety—the most famous of which, *Ônibus 174* (Bus 174) (2002), became one of the most well-known Brazilian documentaries in the US following its screening at Sundance Film Festival. The feature-length film was also applauded at Rotterdam and elected Best Non-Fiction Film at Rio, where it also won the FIPRESCI trophy, awarded by the International Federation of the Film Critics. Padilha's most recent work includes the series *Narcos*, about Pablo Escobar, carried out for the production company and distributor Gaumont, and the 2014 remake of *RoboCop*.

Born in Rio de Janeiro, 1967

1.

2.

3.

1.
Tropa de Elite 2:
O Inimigo Agora É Outro
(Elite Squad 2: The
Enemy Within), 2010

2.
RoboCop, 2014

3.
Tropa de Elite (Elite
Squad), 2007

Fernando Meirelles

After gaining considerable experience as a cameraman through his work on the sitcom *Ernesto Varella, o Repórter*, Fernando Meirelles became one of Latin America's most successful and critically acclaimed directors following the release of *Cidade de Deus* (City of God) in 2002. The film became a global phenomenon. Nominated for the Oscar for Best Director, Meirelles truly popularized the *favela* movie style, in which the camera goes deep inside the Brazilian slums in order to construct a socially-aware narrative. The film was a huge hit in European box offices — especially in London, where it ran for almost five months.

Meirelles had previously directed two feature-length films: the family film *Menino Maluquinho 2: A Aventura* (1998) and *Domesticas* (Maids) (2001). Following the success of *City of God*, he was invited to direct the adaptation of John le Carré's novel *The Constant Gardener*, released in 2005, for which Rachel Weisz won an Oscar for Best Supporting Actress.

Meirelles's more recent work includes a re-telling of José Saramago's *Ensaio Sobre a Cegueira* (Blindness) which was nominated for the Palme d'Or at Cannes Film Festival in 2008, and *360*, a drama starring Jude Law and Anthony Hopkins. Along with directing, Meirelles also owns the production company O2, which has produced noteworthy films such as *Xingu*, by Cao Hamburger.

Born in São Paulo, 1955

```
1–3.
Cidade de Deus
(City of God), 2002

4.
360, 2011

5.
Blindness, 2008
```

1.

2.

3.

4.

5.

Heitor Dhalia

After a successful career in advertising, and just two short films (*A Pantomima da Morte* and *Conceição*) under his belt, Heitor Dahlia decided that his first foray into full-length movie-making should be an ambitious take on one of the most acclaimed pieces of world literature: *Crime and Punishment*, by Fyodor Dostoyevsky. Dahlia used the manuscript to create *Nina*, a piece about the paranoia of people from São Paulo, using the graphic novels of author Lourenço Mutarelli as a visual reference. The film was not particularly successful, but revealed a promising talent.

His next project, *O Cheiro do Ralo* (Drained) (2006), a black comedy that won three awards at the Rio Film Festival, was also inspired by the work of Mutarelli. The film is a metaphor for the moral and political bankruptcy of Brazil, portraying the daily life of an unscrupulous pawn shop owner played by Selton Mello, one of the most sought-after actors in the country.

Dahlia went to Hollywood for the first time in 2012 with the suspense and Hitchcock-esque rhythm of *12 horas* (Gone) (2012), featuring Amanda Seyfried. Back in Brazil, he attempted something more ambitious: the contemporary western *Serra Pelada* (Bald Mountain) (2013), a violent epic about the largest open gold mine in Latin America. Chosen to close the Rio Film Festival, the movie also received a TV adaptation, as a miniseries, shown on the country's largest TV channel, Globo.

Born in Recife, 1970

1–3.
À Deriva (Adrift), 2009

4–6.
Serra Pelada (Bald Mountain), 2013

1.

2.

3.

4.

5.

6.

163

Laís Bodanzky

One of the first successful female directors in Brazilian cinema since the revival of the industry in the 1990s, Laís Bodanzky inherited a passion for film from her father, the director Jorge Bodanzky, who was responsible for the cult classic *Iracema, Uma Transa Amazônica* (1974).

She gained critical acclaim in 2000 for *Bicho de Sete Cabeças* (Brainstorm), her adaptation of the memoir *O Canto dos Malditos* by Brazilian author Austragésilo Carrano, which tells the story of the suffering of a youth interned in a psychiatric hospital after being caught with marijuana by his father. Her first bold move was to cast one of Brazil's most popular *telenovela* (soap opera) stars, Rodrigo Santoro (now a hugely successful Hollywood actor) in the lead role. Applauded despite initial prejudices, Bodanzky left the Brasília Film Festival in 2000 with seven Candango trophies, including those for Best Film, Best Director and Best Actor, awarded to Santoro.

Her next two features, *Chega de Saudade* (The Ballroom) (2007), and *As Melhores Coisas do Mundo* (The Best Things in the World) (2010), also won several awards at Brazilian festivals. The former was seen as a contemporary rereading of Ettore Scola's *Le Bal*, focused on an elderly group's dance ritual. The latter deals with the sexual and emotional adventures of a group of young students in São Paulo. Bodanzky is married to one of the most respected screenplay writers in Brazil, Luiz Bolognesi, who, in 2013, won the top prize at the Annecy Festival with *Uma História de Amor e Fúria*, an animated feature which Bodanzky co-produced.

Born in São Paulo, 1969

1.

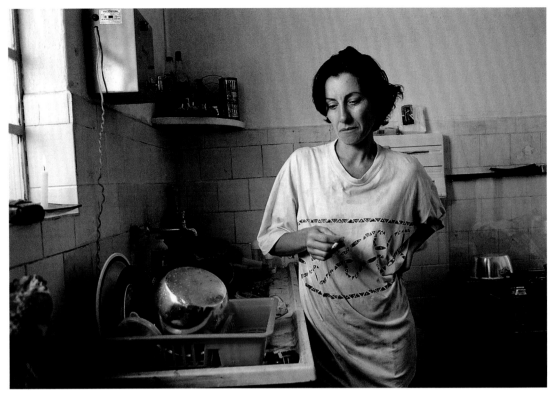

2.

1.
As Melhores Coisas do
Mundo (The Best Things
In The World), 2010

2–3.
Bicho de Sete Cabeças,
(Brainstorm), 2001

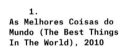

3.

Jorge Furtado

Born in Porto Alegre, in the far south of Brazil, Jorge Furtado discovered that he wanted to be a film-maker whilst studying medicine at University. He abandoned his medical career and transferred to a journalism course on which he could research and write his own films. He is one of the founders of Casa do Cinema de Porto Alegre (Porto Alegre's Cinema House), which was established in 1987 as a producer of independent films and is still successful today.

One of the most versatile Brazilian film-makers, Furtado is recognized both as a director and a writer, and has worked for more than a decade producing series for Globo, Brazil's biggest TV channel.

He first gained recognition after receiving the Silver Bear Award at the Berlin Film Festival in 1989 for his short film *Ilha das Flores* (Isle of Flowers). After that, he moved towards feature-length films, directing *Houve Uma Vez Dois Verões* (Two Summers) (2002), *O Homem Que Copiava* (The Man Who Copied) (2003) and *Meu Tio Matou um Cara* (My Uncle Killed a Guy) (2004).

Despite generally being made on a small budget, Furtado's films are characterized by their witty dialogues, well-directed actors and clever editing.

Born in Porto Alegre, 1959

1.

2.

3.

```
      1.
O Homem Que Copiava
(The Man Who Copied),
2003

      2.
Barbosa, 1988

      3.
Ilha das Flores (Isle
of Flowers), 1990
```

166

Kleber Mendonça Filho

One of the fiercest film critics in Brazil for the last twenty years, famous for his biting irony and fixation on technological innovations, Kleber Mendonça Filho has become one of the pillars of audiovisual production in Pernambuco. As an adolescent, he studied in England, where he became interested in European cinematographic culture. Back in Recife, his home town, he had his first experiences as a video director in the 1990s, experimenting with different genres.

He explored Russian literature in *Vinil Verde* (2004), examined Slavic reality with *Noite de Sexta, Manhã de Sábado* (2006) and in 2009, he released *Recife Frio*. This short film, which tackled climate change in his city, was filmed in a mockumentary style and became a cult favourite.

Influenced by foreign directors such as American John Carpenter and Austrian Michael Haneke, Mendonça Filho made a thriller based on the conflicts of the Pernambuco middle class: *O Som ao Redor* (Neighboring Sounds) won the FIPRESCI prize from the International Federation of Film Critics at its premiere in Rotterdam in 2012. Chosen as one of the best movies of the year by *The New York Times*, the R$2 million (£540,000) production also won him the Redentor trophy for best film at Rio Film Festival and the Kikito trophy for best director at the Gramado Film Festival, along with several other accolades from various countries.

Born in Recife, 1968

1.

3.

1.
O Som ao Redor
(Neighbouring Sounds),
2012

2.
Vinil Verde, 2004

3.
Recife Frio, 2013

Rodrigo Teixeira

One of the most prolific Brazilian producers of the last thirty years, Rio de Janeiro-born Rodrigo Teixeira achieved international fame by pulling off one of the smash hits of the American indie scene in 2013, the comedy *Frances Ha* by Noah Baumbach. He also produced a number of American authors such as Ira Sachs, in *Love is Strange* (2014) and Kelly Reichardt's *Night Moves* (2013).

In Brazil, he had box office success with films such as *Heleno* (2012), the cinematic biography of the football player Heleno de Freitas, played by Rodrigo Santoro, and *Alemão*, a thriller about the drug traffic wars in the Penha neighborhood of Rio de Janeiro, directed by José Eduardo Belmonte (with whom he made *Gorila*, one of the hits of the 2012 Rio de Janeiro Film Festival).

Teixeira began his career in publishing, with the *Camisa 13* book series, in which famous authors wrote about their cherished football teams, and *Amores Expressos*, about Brazilians' experiences abroad. One of Teixeira's books about football inspired the comedy *O Casamento de Romeu e Julieta* (2004), directed by Bruno Barreto. From then on, he began acquiring the rights to novels, stories and comic books to negotiate with directors. Among his projects still in production, the most talked about is the biography of Tim Maia, one of the most popular — and controversial — Brazilian pop singers of all time.

Born in Rio de Janeiro, 1976

1.

1.
Quando Eu Era Vivo,
2014

2.
O Cheiro do Ralo, 2006

3.
Heleno, 2011

4.
Alemão, 2014

2.

3.

4.

169

Karim Aïnouz

A director, videoartist, painter and screenwriter, Karim Aïnouz has won a total of 24 international awards for films shown at the Cannes and Venice film festivals. After working as an assistant director and production assistant on the film *Poison* (1991) by Todd Haynes, he started to direct his own short films in the early 1990s and released his first feature film, *Madame Satã*, in 2002. With a majestic performance from Lázaro Ramos, the film tells the story of a marginalized, homosexual black Brazilian who lived in the Lapa area of Rio de Janeiro in the 1930s. It was highly applauded at Cannes.

Aïnouz's next hit was *O Céu de Suely* (Love for Sale), which revolved around a woman (played by Hermila Guedes) forced to auction her own body in order to support her son. The film was shown at the Venice Film Festival and won the Redentor trophy for best film at the Rio Festival in 2006.

Other successes include *O Abismo Prateado* (The Silver Cliff), a reflection on abandonment inspired by the song 'Olhos nos Olhos' by Chico Buarque, and *Praia do Futuro*, which earned Aïnouz a mention for the Golden Bear award at the Berlin Film Festival, and secured his status as a truly international director. In 2012 he was invited to be a judge for the Cinéfondation and Short Films sections at the Cannes Film Festival.

Born in Fortaleza, 1966

1.
Madame Satã, 2002

2.
O Céu de Suely (Love for Sale), 2006

3.
Viajo Porque Preciso, Volto Porque te Amo (I Travel Because I Have To, I Come Back Because I Love You), 2010

4.
Praia do Futuro, 2014

1.

2.

3.

4.

Daniel Filho

Responsible for triggering an aesthetic revolution in Brazilian TV during the 1970s, Daniel Filho became a Midas of popular cinema in Brazil during the 2000s. He created one blockbuster after another, many adapted from the theatre. The *Se Eu Fosse Você* franchise (2006–09), featuring Tony Ramos and Gloria Pires — famous for their *telenovela* (soap opera) roles, sold more than 9 million tickets.

An actor during the 1960s, when he worked on seminal projects of the *Cinema Novo* period, such as *Os Cafajestes* (The Unscrupulous Ones) (1962) by Ruy Guerra and *Boca de Ouro* (The Golden Mouth) (1963) by Nelson Pereira dos Santos, Daniel Filho cemented himself as a director in 1969 by filming *Pobre Príncipe Encantado*, a romantic comedy featuring the successful

singer Wanderley Cardoso. Since then, he has continued directing for both cinema and TV, and become known for his snappy dialogue and concise plots.

He directed pieces on the post-hippie youth, such as *O Casal* (1975) and a children's film, *O Cangaceiro Trapalhão* (1983). In the second half of the 1980s and the 1990s, he concentrated on producing, working on *Cidade de Deus* (City of God) (2002), amongst others. He returned to directing with *A Partilha* (The Inheritance), in 2001, based on the play by Miguel Falabella, and, since then, has released another eight features, almost always breaking the 1 million ticket mark at the box office.

Born in Rio de Janeiro, 1937

1.

1.
Tempos de Paz (Time
of Peace), 2009

2.
Muito Gelo e Dois Dedos
D'Água, 2006

3.
A Dona da História
(Owner of the Story),
2004

4.
Muito Gelo e Dois Dedos
D'Água, 2006

2.

3.

4.

Roberta Sudbrack

Thiago & Felipe Castanho

Alex Atala

Helena Rizzo

Alberto Landgraf

Rodrigo Oliveira

Rafael Mantesso

food

This is the hour for Brazilian chefs. It took a long time to arrive, but it is finally here. More aware than ever of their social role and of the rich pantry that they have at their disposal, they explore national ingredients like never before, searching for wonderful and flavourful dishes, contributing not only to projecting an attractive image of the country abroad but also to captivating Brazilians themselves. There has never been so much talk about Brazilian gastronomy, and the issue now occupies an unprecedented central role in people's lives. This is hardly surprising, as the diversity is fascinating: to taste wines in the garage wineries of Rio Grande do Sul and then take a plane some 5,000 miles (8,000 km) north to try *tucupi* (a sauce prepared with cassava liquid that has been fermented and boiled) in the forests of Pará is like travelling to another continent.

The path of discovery was opened by European chefs, arriving in Brazil from the 1970s onwards, who disseminated classical culinary techniques, and was paved by Brazilians such as Alex Atala and Roberta Sudbrack, tireless researchers of the best that Brazil has to offer. Now, a third generation led by young chefs such as Helena Rizzo, brothers Thiago and Felipe Castanho, Rodrigo Oliveira and Alberto Landgraf, has taken into its hands the challenge of redefining Brazilian cuisine for the world. Although *feijoada* (stew made with black beans and pork cuts, served with rice, kale, sliced orange and pork chops), the *caipirinha* (cocktail made with *cachaça*, lime and sugar) and *churrasco* (Brazilian-style barbecue) are known globally, Brazil's gastronomy is not as easily identifiable by its ingredients and typical dishes as other cuisines such as Italian and Chinese — at least not until now. There is no shortage of products, but Brazil needs to invest in more research and more experimentation.

A compelling example comes from the Amazon — and the city of Belém, more precisely — where the Castanho family runs the restaurants Remanso do Peixe and Remanso do Bosque. The former, opened in 2011 by the family patriarch, Francisco, and today led by brothers Thiago and Felipe, maintains in its menu traditional dishes with regional ingredients, such as *tucupi, jambu* (a flowering herb that produces a tingling, numbing sensation), chilli, fish and fruit. Bubbling in earthenware pans, the restaurant's fragrant *caldeiradas* (fish stews) are a singular experience.

In Remanso do Bosque, launched in 2011, the brothers decided to go beyond the traditional, researching the flavours of the forest to offer a more creative, product-oriented cuisine. They brought in interesting products, such as the chocolate produced in the neighbouring Amazonian island Combu, and invented concoctions that surprise even the *Paraenses* (residents of Pará state), such as açaí flour, and couscous made of *farinha d'água* (literally 'water flour', made from cassava softened by river water) hydrated with coconut milk. To boost creativity, in the second floor of the restaurant they installed a lab for testing new possibilities — RemansoLab — where they have developed, amongst other things, a type of crackling made from the skin of the *pirarucu* (a large freshwater fish). It took the brothers two months of experimentation to arrive at the exact crunchiness they were looking for. They are also cataloguing flours from all over the country, having amassed a collection that already includes over 50 different types. The relevance of their work has travelled far, and Remanso do Bosque now occupies the thirty-eighth place in the list of Latin America's 50 Best Restaurants, as published by *Restaurant* magazine.

About 1,500 miles (2,500 km) south of Belém, the immense and diverse city of São Paulo forms the epicentre of a Brazilian gastronomy revolution. In addition to the obvious reference, Alex Atala's restaurant D.O.M. (the main exponent of Brazilian gastronomy in the world), the city has many important

1.
Traditional fruit stall
in northern Brazil

2.
Fisherman in the Amazon
region

3.
Preparing fish in the
Amazon region

1.

2.

3.

talents, all dedicated to the serious flavour research required to consolidate Brazilian contemporary cuisine. Among them is Helena Rizzo, originally from Rio Grande do Sul, who commands Maní's kitchen with Spanish chef Daniel Redondo, her husband. She could have been an architect, but decided to leave the profession to dive into gastronomy. She interned with some of the best chefs in São Paulo but had her defining experience in El Celler de Can Roca, where Redondo built part of his career.

Opened in 2006, Maní's acclaim has only grown since then, peaking with its entry into *Restaurant* magazine's international ranking and, in 2014, when its award of Best Female Chef in Latin America was granted to Rizzo. With only a 70-seat capacity and a discrete entrance in the upper class Jardins region of the city, Maní offers techno-emotional food. National ingredients are very important in the restaurant's dishes, but not necessarily the only stars. They shine alongside eastern products and Catalan recipes, for example. Spherical *feijoada* has become a house classic. Its kitchen also impresses with cold *jabuticaba* (round, black-skinned, white-pulped, berry-like fruit) soup, served with pickled cauliflower and shrimp steamed in *cachaça* vapour, as well as with its cassava served with *tucupi*, coconut milk and olive oil infused with white truffle.

Another inevitable reference is Mocotó, a restaurant opened decades ago in a neighbourhood at the opposite end of the scale from the luxury of Jardins, which has gained recognition as a gourmet destination. Rodrigo Oliveira—the son of José de Almeida, a former migrant worker from Pernambuco, who established the restaurant in the 1970s—took over from his father in 2004, retaining the northeastern Brazilian theme of the menu, but aiming to update the preparation techniques, and thus improve the quality of the food. This is not the northeastern cuisine that tourists are used to eating in the coastal areas, but rather *sertanejo* food from the semi-arid rural regions, where *carne de sol* (jerk beef), pork innards, beans and broad beans, cassava and *queijo de coalho* (curdled cheese) feature prominently. With its attractive prices, an extensive *cachaça* menu and portions of many sizes, Mocotó secured itself a long list of loyal patrons, who will often join the long queues to get in the door.

According to Oliveira, Brazil will have a great cuisine once regional food is better understood throughout the country. Having conquered not only the public, but also the media, winning many awards with his unfussy cuisine based on the food culture of Pernambuco's countryside, Oliveira knows what he is talking about. Among his most famous dishes are his *caldo de mocotó* (cow's hoof broth), the *mocofava* (cow's hoof broth with broad beans), *baião de dois* (a casserole made of rice, beans, curdled cheese, sausage, bacon and jerk beef) and *carne de sol* (jerk beef). After taking over Mocotó, Oliveira improved the preparation of the *carne de sol* so as to make it more succulent. It is salted, matured under controlled temperatures, dried in a greenhouse, vacuum-sealed, cooked in low temperatures and finished off in the oven. Rodrigo also invents his own recipes in the *sertanejo* spirit—his tapioca cubes with curdled cheese being one of the most successful. In 2013, he opened Esquina Mocotó in a neighbouring house in order to develop traditional dishes from other Brazilian regions.

A more recent revelation in São Paulo, Alberto Landgraf—a chef of German and Japanese origin—has been gaining prestige for his restaurant Epice, opened in 2011. The awards came fast and, like Mocotó, his restaurant was classified as one of Latin America's 50 Best Restaurants. He makes food that is extremely difficult to conceive and prepare, but still familiar to those who eat it. He makes everything that is served in the restaurant (including the

4.
Seriguela fruit

5.
Jabuticaba fruit

4.

5.

bread and the ice cream), usually championing undervalued ingredients such as pork ears, which he serves with mustard and fried kale.

Landgraf's style is natural and minimal. It is a kind of cuisine in which technique, presentation, crockery and service play supporting roles, while the star is unquestionably the ingredients — their flavours preserved and highlighted. It is a brave choice. Ingredients appear as they are, fresh, without sauces or spices to mask them: 'I don't season the foods I use,' he explains, 'my goal is simply to enhance their flavour'. Presentation is clean and the flavour is intense. Notable highlights in his menu are the pickled onions with tapioca and peanuts, the raw nuts ice cream and the shank with cold bone marrow, all meticulously prepared. Alex Atala considers Landgraf one of the five best chefs in Brazil, believing that more than just being an excellent cook, Landgraf plays a social role, both through his training of the young people who work with him and by his commitment to relevant events and gastronomical movements.

And commitment is a concept that no serious Brazilian chef working today can neglect. The country's chefs are playing a new role in society, beginning with their awareness of the fact that they are a link between good producers and consumers. Small producers, above all, depend on this link. With this heightened awareness, chefs must dictate the trends, balancing excellence and sustainability. Brazil is a country of monocultures and commodities, with large crops of a few products: soy crops, coffee crops, cattle pastures and rice plantations. This mass production is organized and controlled by big businesses and cooperatives, and survival outside of this system is rare. New products are still not absorbed well by the market and their producers are not granted incentives by the government; boycotted by potential partners, it is rare for restaurants to take an interest in them. Unfortunately, there are only a few examples of producers that have diverted from the standard path, taken risks to make things differently and open up the market.

There is one success story that is worth telling: the story of Chicão Ruzene. Ruzene, son and grandson of rice farmers, planted white rice for 23 years, as did (and still do) most farmers from the region of the Paraíba river valley, in São Paulo state. He knew that he was just another cog in the machine of the rice commodity market, and at a certain point he decided that he no longer wanted to be. After meeting Cândido Ricardo Bastos — a researcher from the Agronomic Institute of Campinas who, at the time, had a project to develop special types of rice — Ruzene started planting black rice, despite not having a list of potential buyers. He was a visionary, though he did not know it at the time.

Chef Alex Atala discovered the operation, and before long was buying Ruzene's black rice for his own restaurant D.O.M. Today, Ruzene packages his production for high-end supermarkets and at least eight small businesses. And it is not only black rice he produces: he also plants red, *cateto*, basmati and Arborio rice varieties, as well as a curious type of mini rice. In addition, he has built a small lab for developing rice, a crop for testing more than a hundred special types of rice, and founded a small cooperative with ten other small rice farmers in Pindamonhagaba — where his rented crop is also located.

Atala advised chef André Mifano to take a similar risk. After getting to know Mifano and his tireless approach to his work, Atala advised him to invest in cured meats and cold cuts. Mifano started his career at 18, washing dishes. He quickly realized that cooking was his vocation. He studied in London, spent some time in kitchens in San Francisco, went back to São Paulo and in 2008 opened Vito — a restaurant that seated only 28 people in Vila Beatriz, a neighbourhood with well-off residents but few gastronomic options, in the western region of the city. The small restaurant today occupies a larger house (seating 45 patrons), but Mifano is as faithful as ever to his philosophy of producing himself a large part of what is on the menu and saving as much energy as possible. He does not use tablecloths, in order to save water, soap and energy. He also tries to buy everything that he serves within a 93-mile (150 km) radius from his restaurant and gives preference to organic produce. A lover of conspiracy theories, Mifano also started to work on preparations that save energy. For him, the opposite of raw is not only cooked, but also cured and fermented. And it is in the production of cured meats that he invests most of his time.

Today, Mifano produces over 30 varieties of cured meats and cold cuts and was the first to develop versions of salami and coppa made of *queixada* (white-lipped peccary—a Brazilian swine). His artisanal work has been featured both in the international and national media, which has also granted him awards. Atala is also considering producing a line of products with Mifano.

Good intentions and good ingredients can encounter obstacles that are almost impossible to overcome in Brazil. This is often due to out-dated laws, bureaucracy and a total disinterest on the part of the government. The artisanal cheeses made in Minas Gerais from raw milk are an example: their production is considered part of Brazil's national heritage by the Instituto do Patrimônio Histórico e Artístico Nacional (Institute of National Artistic and Historical Heritage), but only recently have discussions begun on the possibility of selling them outside their native state. Submitted to the same rules imposed on large industries and out-dated sanitary legislation, the small producers of the most well-known Brazilian cheese were almost wiped out, however, the increasing demand from chefs and gourmands for this unique product has helped preserve it. Today, even though it is much more expensive than similar industrialized cheeses, artisanal Minas cheese is much sought after.

A similar situation plagues the honey made by native Brazilian bees, which, also due to out-dated legislation, cannot be called honey. Only honey made by European and African bees, introduced to Brazil centuries ago, can officially be labelled such. The genuine Brazilian honey, produced by bee species such as *uruçu, mandaçaia, tiúba* and *jataí* is less sweet, more watery and has a light touch of acidity that makes it special and different from industrialized honeys. Yet, according to the regulations set by the Brazilian government, it is not honey, because it does not conform to prevalent quality control parameters allowing only for the use of honey from African bees.

This situation is of special concern for Brazil, particularly as the country has a climate that is extremely favourable for the production of honey from native species and is home to the greatest diversity of stingless bees in the world (more than 200 species) rendering what is potentially an enormous asset only partially exploited. Nearly all of the honey produced in Brazil still comes from African bees. The productivity of Brazilian bees is lower, but the honey they produce is sold at a higher price in the market. Additionally, these specialist honeys can mature and eventually be harvested. In this frustrating scenario, the Associação dos Criadores de Abelhas Nativas (Association of Native Beekeepers) of Guaraqueçaba, in Paraná, emerges as a beacon of resistance and hope. It consists of 25 families of small producers who organized themselves to improve their production, processing and retail operations.

The Brazilian government has not yet identified a need for investing in gastronomy or, if it has, it has not yet embraced the great marketing opportunities that this could provide. Society, on the other hand, is starting to move. Gastronomic festivals are getting more politicized, the public is more and more informed (there is an increasing number of magazines, TV shows and blogs dedicated to the issue) and NGOs, institutes and other entities with the common goal of advancing Brazilian gastronomy are starting to emerge. Notable examples are Sertãobras, Centro de Cultura Culinária Câmara Cascudo (the Câmara Cascudo Centre for Culinary Culture), Conspiração Gastronômica and the Instituto ATÁ, co-founded by Alex Atala.

Opened in 2013, Instituto ATÁ is the result of a collaboration between Atala and a group of sociologists, anthropologists, journalists, environmentalists and advertisers to 'bring knowing and eating, eating and cooking, cooking and producing, producing and nature closer to each other'. Its ambitious goal is to improve the supply chain of native ingredients such as the chilli mixture made by the Baniwa natives in the Rio Negro region, vanilla from the *Cerrado* (a tropical biome in central Brazil) and honey from native bees. Their actions include attempts to raise awareness of the value of Brazilian oils, such as *pequi* (from the *Caryocar brasiliense* tree) avocado, jackfruit and *patauá* (from two species of palm), and aid understanding of biomes and their infinite ingredients. According to Atala, Instituto ATÁ will be an observatory of public and private food policies. 'We cannot forget that the resources coming from the sea, from the forest, from the countryside are finite. We cannot forget that, before the pans, comes the man who needs help,' he states.

It is impossible to speak of Brazilian gastronomy without mentioning Atala, who opened his restaurant D.O.M. in 1999. Serving high-quality food based on the country's best ingredients, especially from the Amazon region, *Restaurant* magazine ranked it fourth out of the World's 50 Best Restaurants. Ten years later, he opened Dalva & Dito (inspired by Brazilian traditional home cooking) and, in 2013, he reopened the famous Riviera bar, an icon of São Paulo's bohemian scene.

Atala is a fierce advocate both of championing regional cuisine and supporting small producers. In his restaurants he partners with some of the suppliers who sell him high-quality ingredients as a result of fair trade and environmentally concerned practice. More than learning where each ingredient comes from and how his suppliers and producers are doing, he is intent on using gastronomy as a tool for social, environmental and cultural transformation. Atala knows better than anyone, how to use this for the benefit of Brazilian gastronomy — never before has Brazilian cuisine enjoyed as much visibility, both inside and outside the country, as it does today.

Europeans such as Claude Troisgros, Emmanuel Bassoleil and Laurent Suaudeau, who arrived in Brazil after the 1970s to work in restaurants, opened the eyes of Brazilians to their own gastronomic wealth, which, until then, had been woefully undervalued. They have also contributed immensely to the dissemination of classical culinary techniques, and Atala's generation consolidated this work using Brazil's fruit, roots, fish and chillis. In addition to Atala, names such as Mara Salles (of Tordesilhas, in São Paulo), Flávia Quaresma (of now-closed Carême, in Rio de Janeiro) and Paulo Martins (ambassador of Pará's cuisine with his Lá em Casa, which closed in 2010) stand out.

Another name in this group that deserves special attention is Roberta Sudbrack, who runs her eponymous restaurant in Rio de Janeiro. Tasting one of her recipes, such as smoked okra stuffed with semi-cooked shrimp, one might think that she had learned her techniques throughout Europe, interning in starred restaurants worldwide, but although the chef began her training abroad, she is virtually self-taught. Sudbrack's early days started with a hot dog stand in Brasília and catering for small dinners in private residences until

6.
Catupiry cheese

7.
Jambu leaves

8.
Brazilian honey

6.

7.

8.

she met the former President Fernando Henrique Cardoso who invited her to take over the kitchens of the federal government headquarters, Palácio da Alvorada, where she stayed for seven years.

Sudbrack, a native of Rio Grande do Sul, creates minimalist recipes, involving no more than three elements, all with their essential flavour preserved and highlighted. In a small orange house near Lagoa Rodrigo de Freitas, Roberta serves a few people every night. Her tables are some of the most coveted in Rio de Janeiro and must be reserved well in advance. The tasting menu, with nine courses, uses ingredients chosen the day that they are to be used. She selects the best meats and the freshest fish.

It may take a while longer, but the future points to an ever greater number of consumers searching for products carrying indicators of quality (in a broad, not exclusively gastronomic sense), such as certifications of origin. This has already become a reality in the Brazilian drinks industry—with coffee, *cachaça* and beer, mainly—and is becoming increasingly important to the Brazilian gourmet when buying domestic cheeses, meats and chocolate. Fruit and nuts have also received attention, especially when used in ice creams and desserts. Never before have ingredients such as *pequi, buriti* (from the *Mauritia flexuosa* palm tree) and *baru* (the toasted pit, or almond, from a fruit of the *Dipteryx alata* tree) or açaí and Brazil nuts from the Amazon, been so valued. Soon, the same shall happen with fish from Brazilian rivers, still underused in restaurant kitchens. There are chefs who are already exchanging salmon for smoked *surubim* (from the catfish family) and the popularity of other freshwater fish such as *tambaquis, dourados* and *tucunarés* is only likely to increase.

The diversity of these ingredients indicates the gastronomic wealth of Brazil, an enormous country with territories that do not necessarily coincide with the political divisions on the map. To shed light on this, it is worth mentioning sociologist Carlos Alberto Dória's theory of discontinued culinary shades. Dória, one of the foremost thinkers of Brazilian gastronomy today, suggests that instead of states, Brazil could be divided into the following culinary regions: Amazonian, coastal (from Ceará to Espírito Santo), Bahian, Southern (divided into *pequi, mate* and *pinhão*) and *caipira*, or rural (including Minas Gerais, São Paulo and part of the central-western region).

Dória's proposal reinforces the characteristics of each region, uniting towns and cities according to their affinity to ingredients and cuisines while also being aware of divisions between existing territories. Thiago Castanho, for example, has complained about how difficult it is to sell pork in his restaurants in Belém, where inhabitants eat more river fish than in Minas Gerais, the land of pork lovers. Try to make *pão de queijo* (cheese bread) in Porto Alegre and you will realize how it is virtually impossible to find a semi-matured Minas cheese to incorporate into the dough. And eating meat as good, and as cheap, as in Rio Grande do Sul's capital city is an unlikely possibility outside of it, while feasts of inebriating fruit are only possible in the northeastern coast or in the Amazon.

Among the vast variety of ingredients present in Brazil, cassava is the strongest candidate for the country's symbol of national cuisine. Present from the north to the south, one can obtain many sub-products from it that can be used in countless recipes. Fried, boiled, roasted or made into a purée, this noble root can appear on any plate, from starters to desserts, and in the most diverse main dishes.

As was the case with the greatest gastronomic powers of the world, Brazil is starting to rediscover its ingredients. In each part of the country, one can encounter candidates to become stars as bright as cassava. People are

9.
Brazilian maniuara ants

10.
Araçá-boi fruit

starting to become more interested in gastronomy, the economy is favourable, and the government is starting to see that gastronomy is an important sector for social, cultural and even economic transformations. The number of professionals working in the trade is increasing daily, as is the level of professionalism within the industry. There are more and more interesting places to eat. Events organized in Brazil attract media and chefs from around the world, all eager to explore this country of continental proportions. This is a rediscovery of Brazil—and it starts in the kitchen.

9.

10.

Roberta Sudbrack

It was in Washington D.C., whilst studying to become a veterinary surgeon, that Roberta Sudbrack discovered that she wanted to become a chef. She ended up living with her grandparents in Brasília learning how to make stews and sauces, and even spending time selling hot dogs on the street, but soon began to cook for small events in the federal capital.

At one such event in 1997, then-president Fernando Henrique Cardoso was in attendance and asked to meet the chef. His wife, first lady Ruth Cardoso, had for some time wanted to improve the quality of the dishes served at the presidential residence. Sudbrack soon found herself running the kitchen of the Palácio da Alvorada for the presidential couple. Her mission was to bring to the table the best of Brazilian cuisine, using the best Brazilian ingredients, without offending the demanding—and sensitive—palates of heads of state from around the world.

Sudbrack asked to leave her position when Fernando Henrique ended his presidency—she wanted her own restaurant. To that end she relocated to Rio de Janeiro and opened her eponymous bistro on the edge of the Rodrigo de Freitas Lagoon. It soon became a gourmet landmark, won several national awards and now features on *Restaurant* magazine's 50 Best list. Sudbrack makes a point of always being in the kitchen and chooses fresh ingredients for the menu herself. For that reason, she argues, she can't expand her restaurant.

Born in Porto Alegre, 1968

1.

1.
Marinated heart of
palm, prawn, hillbilly
egg and aïoli

2.
Burrata cheese with
tomato filet

3.
Ojo de bife (ribeye)
with béarnaise sauce
and banana sour

2.

3.

Thiago & Felipe Castanho

One of Alex Atala's main achievements has been to show that Brazilian cuisine goes far beyond the typical Rio-São Paulo axis, in particular highlighting the gastronomy of the Amazon region. But it was brothers Thiago and Felipe Castanho that put the city of Belém on the country's culinary map: their combination of incredible cooking, exciting ingredients and unique ambiance started to draw attention to the capital of Pará, in the north of Brazil.

The two began in the food business by delivering pizzas for their father Francisco, and later working in his restaurant Remanso do Peixe in Belém, which specializes in freshwater fish. Attracted by new culinary schools, they both decided to enrol in a gastronomy course at Campos do Jordão, in São Paulo state (although at different times). After his studies, Thiago spent time in Lisbon, working as an apprentice for chef Vitor Sobral.

Today, the brothers manage two restaurants, Remanso do Peixe, opened by their father, and Remanso do Bosque. Regional ingredients, including annatto, arapaima, wild mushrooms and local nuts are the restaurants' top features, always prepared in an original way and with cutting-edge techniques. Thiago is more involved with the day-to-day activities and researching new ingredients. Felipe is his brother's right-hand man, but recently has been more involved with the dining experience, service and harmonizing the dishes and beverage offerings.

Thiago: born in Belém, 1987
Felipe: born in Belém, 1989

1.
Bacuri with sago and
coffee

2.
Mango with manioc flour

3.
Pupunha palm with rice
crunch

4.
Cupuaçu jelly with
Combú cocoa

1.

2.

3.

4.

Alex Atala

Alex Atala is undoubtedly the biggest name in Brazilian gastronomy today, but it was by chance that Milad Alexandre Mack Atala became a chef. To obtain a student visa that would enable him to stay in Europe, he signed up for a gastronomy course at Namur University in Belgium. There he discovered that he had skills in the kitchen, and later, when he was hired to decide upon and prepare a daily menu for a restaurant in Milan, he decided that cooking was his calling.

Back in Brazil, he settled in São Paulo and worked as a chef at the restaurants Sushi Pasta and Filomena. In 1999, he opened his first place, Namesa, and at the end of that same year, together with two partners, he launched D.O.M. restaurant, named after an acronym for the Latin phrase *Deo Optimo Maximo* (To the greatest and best god). The success of its recipes prepared with 100 per cent local produce made Atala discover his mission: to champion regional Brazilian ingredients. And he was well equipped for that — he was an experienced hunter and fisherman and knew the Brazilian fauna and flora well, having explored the Amazon, the central plain and the Atlantic rainforest numerous times. He brought all of that knowledge to his restaurant's menu.

With D.O.M., Atala began to collect awards. In 2006, the restaurant appeared in the World's 50 Best list by *Restaurant* magazine and by 2012 it had climbed to 4th place. In 2009, Atala opened Dalva & Dito, a restaurant serving traditional Brazilian cuisine with a gastronomic twist. Along with the impeccable cooking, the restaurant also became famous for the *galhinada* (chicken stew) invented by Atala's sous-chef, Geovane Carneiro, which is served in the early hours between Saturday night and Sunday morning, accompanied by live music from Brazilian bands.

Currently, Atala's work goes way beyond what he plates for D.O.M.'s customers. Via numerous activities throughout the country and the Instituto ATÁ, he is seeking to raise the profile — and improve the use — of Brazilian ingredients, whilst protecting the environment and improving quality of life for Brazilians.

Born in São Bernardo do Campo, 1968

1.
Lightly toasted black rice with green vegetables and brazil nut milk

2.
Lime and banana ravioli

1.

191

2.

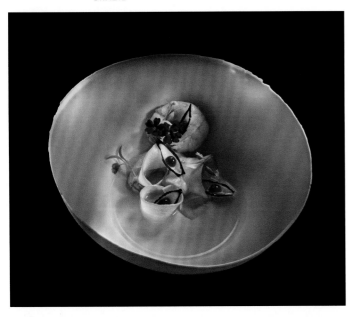

3.

4.

5.

3.
Cajuína, prawn, pickled
chayote, onion and
tamarind purée

4.
Coconut apple with
seaweed, turnip, radish
and cumaru vinaigrette

5.
Wild boar with plantain
purée and aromatic
pepper farofa

6.
Heart of palm
fettuccine with butter,
sage, Parmesan cheese
and popcorn powder

6.

Helena Rizzo

Helena Rizzo was elected the World's Best Female Chef by *Restaurant* magazine in 2014: the first time a Brazilian has ever claimed the title. In 2012, her restaurant Maní, which she opened in 2004 and runs together with her husband, the talented Spanish chef Daniel Redondo, featured on their list of the 50 best in the world. Before becoming a chef, Helena trained as an architect and also worked as a fashion model, but when she moved to São Paulo she discovered a connection with food and an aptitude for cooking.

In 1997 she began to work with the chef Emmanuel Bassoleil at the restaurant Roanne, before spending four years in Europe: first in Italy, and later, Spain, where she was an apprentice at several restaurants until joining the team at El Celler de Can Roca, alongside chef Joan Roca and his two brothers Jordi and Josep. From El Celler

she went on to become the appetizer chef at Roca Moo restaurant at Hotel Omm in Barcelona, also run by the Roca brothers. After a year there, Rizzo decided to return to Brazil and open her own restaurant together with her friend, television presenter Fernanda Lima.

Maní soon became a point of reference on the São Paulo and Brazilian gastronomic circuits, famous for dishes such as baked *manioca* with coconut milk and *tucupi* froth and a clever interpretation of *feijoada*, Brazil's national dish, in which Rizzo creates 'beans' from the concentrated essence of the dish, sealed in a bubble of gelatine to look like beans themselves.

Born in Porto Alegre, 1978

1.

1.
Cashew ceviche

2.
Marrow with pupunha,
açaí, spinach and
mustard vinaigrette

3.
Butterfly ginger mille-
feuille with mango and
butterfly ginger flower
sorbet

4.
Beef cheeks with marrow
and taioba purée

2.

3.

4.

5.

6.

7.

5.
Caruru — okra, caramel
cashew nuts, aviú
(small freshwater
shrimp) and dendê oil

6.
Catch of the day with
grilled sweet potatoes
and red onions, curdled
goat's milk and
homemade Spanish oil

7.
Coconut panna cotta
with rum and white
chocolate ice cream,
pineapple pearls over
a lemongrass and
pineapple consommé

8.
Cheese flan from Serra
da Canastra with dulce
de leche, dry araruta
biscuits and guava
sorbet

8.

Alberto Landgraf

Alberto Landgraf's culinary career began in London in the year 2000: a short trip to the UK to perfect his English became a five year visit and it was there that he discovered he wanted to be a chef. Half Japanese, half German, Landgraf studied gastronomy at Westminster Kingsway College and was an apprentice for some of the biggest names on the London dining scene, such as Gordon Ramsay and Tom Aikens. He also spent time in France, working with Pierre Gagnaire.

Back in Brazil, he established himself in São Paulo and worked for the Companhia Tradicional de Comércio, one of the most successful non-gastronomic enterprises in the country. In 2011, Landgraf decided to open his own restaurant, Epice, an intimate space with room for just 28 diners, in Jardins, an elegant neighborhood of São Paulo. In putting together his clever menu, he was cautious: seeking lightness in his food, he uses few carbohydrates — risottos and pasta don't feature at Epice — and Landgraf explores different cuts and uses for each ingredient. Everything served at the restaurant

(from bread to ice cream) is made in his kitchen, from fresh seasonal ingredients, and he takes great care over every aspect of the presentation: from the china to the accompaniments.

Landgraf only hires very junior chefs, preferring to promote from within, making a point to open up spots for new professionals coming out of the new culinary courses recently launched in Brazil. Unsurprisingly he has caught the attention of Alex Atala, who cites him as a great chef, and he has already been elected one of the best new chefs by the top national publications on the topic. In 2012, he was named amongst Latin America's 50 Best Restaurants by *Restaurant* magazine.

Born in Cornélio Procópio, 1980

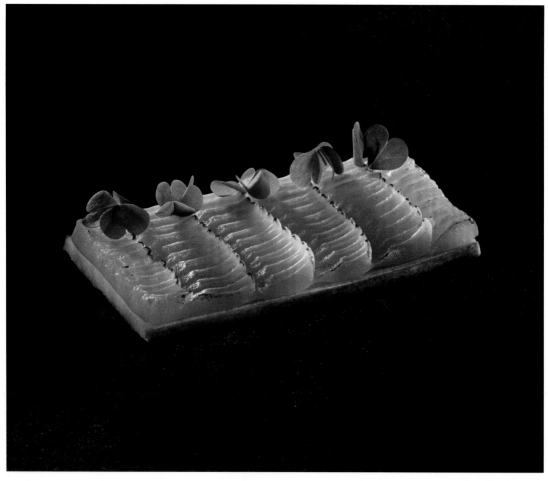

1.
Marinated squid with
abobrinha wood sorrel

2.
Pickled mackerel with
lemon purée

3.
Cured pork belly with
dried manioc and
toasted cashew nut

1.

2.

3.

4.

5.

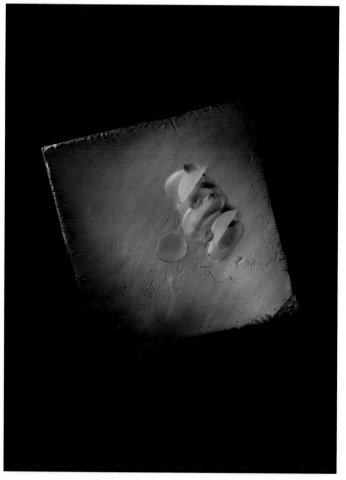

6.

4.
Braised leeks, mussel
emulsion, tucupi and
sorrel oil

5.
Red onions, tapioca,
peanut and sugar cane
vinegar

6.
Pupunha heart of palm
with fermented pear and
Jataí honey

7.
Grouper head pirão with
biquinho chilli and
puffed mini rice

Rodrigo Oliveira

After ten years running the kitchen at Mocotó restaurant, Rodrigo Oliveira has become famous in the Vila Medeiros district of São Paulo where he works and is now considered one of the best chefs in Brazil, but in his own neighbourhood many still refer to him simply as 'Zé's kid'.

Originally from the state of Pernambuco, Zé opened a shop in Vila Medeiros where he sold products from the north and northeast of Brazil such as top-shelf *cachaça* and sun-dried beef. Over time, he started to offer food and drink to his clientele, and so the shop received a makeover, becoming well known for its simple menu and high-quality drinks. Oliveira helped out at the shop and, during the holidays, visited his father's side of the family in the rural northeast.

The influence of these trips is evident in his dishes, which he now serves at Mocotó. After studying gastronomy, Oliveira took over the kitchen at the shop's small bar and with the techniques he learned in college, he transformed the typical cuisine of the northeast into attractive and contemporary dishes.

The restaurant now employs a number of local residents who previously had to travel great distances to earn their living. Many of the ingredients he uses are sourced on his constant travels to visit family and discover new people and places. Oliveira has won all of Brazil's most important culinary awards and is on *Restaurant* magazine's list of the top 50 Latin American restaurants.

Born in São Paulo, 1980

1.

1.
Brazilian rice and
beans with curdled
cheese, sausage, bacon
and jerk beef

2.
Creamy manioc purée
with jerk beef and
cream cheese filling
and grated cheese
topping

3.
Cubes of tapioca with
curdled cheese and
bittersweet chilli
sauce

4.
Banana, cheese, sugar,
farofa and cinnamon

5.
Crispy pork rinds

6.
Lamb stew with manioc,
cherry tomatoes,
olives, spring onion
and parsley

2.

3.

4.

5.

6.

Daniel Trench & Celso Longo

Elaine Ramos

Yomar Augusto

Kiko Farkas

Rico Lins

Paulo Werneck

graphic design

Some of the most interesting experiments in graphic design have emerged from a country that, fifteen years ago, still very much occupied the periphery of visual culture. Since then, there have been posters made using techniques from silkscreen to digital printing, books printed on the same paper used to make bus tickets, and book covers printed on ultra-resistant material (think FedEx envelopes) or printed with a huge wooden letterpress, silk-screened and then photocopied. In this interval, Brazilian graphic design has bloomed on an international level, secured its own place in the country's culture, and gained a new-found independence from other areas, such as architecture and advertising, under whose brackets it previously fell. Bold, expensive projects, which would have been unthinkable a few years ago, are now routinely developed. Designers from all over the world have turned their eyes to Brazil and its young graphic culture, and Brazilian designers have finally achieved international acclaim without having to move abroad. This 'graphic Renaissance' is arguably the most important moment for design in Brazil since the 1950s, when the first Brazilian design schools were opened under the rigorous rationalist principles of the Bauhaus and Ulm School of Design.

Education in the second half of the twentieth century was scarred by the civil-military dictatorship (1964–85), which stifled the country's cultural production. Yet it was a time of great effervescence in all artistic fields. Conceptually, national design was going through an important formative period, reaping the fruits of the pioneering work of the São Paulo Museum of Modern Art (MAM-SP, 1948) and the Escola Superior de Desenho Industrial (ESDI, 1963), the country's first industrial design school, whose foundations are seen as milestones in national graphic history. Before the 1950s, the word 'design' did not even feature in Brazilian dictionaries. As historian Rafael Cardoso describes, 'At that time, what emerged was not design per se [...] but the awareness of design as a concept, as a profession and as an ideology.' That is, design as we understand it today.

This new culture grew deep roots in the country and produced masters such as Aloísio Magalhães and Alexandre Wollner, who forged a great portion of Brazilian visual communications in the second half of the twentieth century. It was within this environment, where the aesthetics of the Ulm School ruled, that Rico Lins graduated from ESDI in the 1970s. Although taught by Wollner, Lins's work appeared to be a radical denial of the clean lines and economy of means prescribed by his professors, as if the lesson had been learned upside down. Lins was one of the first of a generation educated under the influence of *tropicalismo*, the cultural movement led by Caetano Veloso and Gilberto Gil, which, from 1967 on, has spread from music and fine arts to all fields of Brazilian culture. A kind of reversal of bossa nova — the opposite of its cleanness, clarity and elegance — *tropicalismo* imposed itself as the last great cultural force in Brazil.

The Brazil of the *tropicalistas* was pop, kitsch, strident, sentimental and deeply honest in its contradictions. It was at the same time a denunciation of the modernization project promoted by the military dictatorship and a loving criticism of bossa nova's utopias. Still marked by backwardness, poverty, illiteracy and countless social injustices, the country no longer seemed to fit into the idyllic representations of the 1950s Modernism. In the field of graphic design, Rogério Duarte was the main representative of *tropicalismo*, having designed the poster for Glauber Rocha's 1964 film *Deus e o Diabo na Terra do Sol* (Black God, White Devil) which became an iconic image for 1960s Brazil. Through the lenses of *tropicalismo*, Modernism and backwardness overlap in the same country, in the same poster, in the same book, as if they are layers

1.
Deus e o Diablo na
Terra do Sol (Black
God, White Devil) film
poster by Rogério
Duarte, 1964

1.

in a permanent conflict and an intriguing harmony—just like the lyrics of its musical manifestos 'Alegria, Alegria', by Caetano Veloso and 'Domingo no Parque', by Gilberto Gil. Aesthetically, the notions of juxtaposition and montage gained prominence, to the detriment of Modernist composition.

Implicit or not, this tension is visible in the work of contemporary graphic designers as diverse as Rico Lins, Elaine Ramos, Kiko Farkas, Daniel Trench, Celso Longo, Guto Lacaz and Gustavo Piqueira. But what makes these artists 'Brazilian', and what common traces can we find in such different works? It could be argued that 'Brazilian-ness' may lie less in the docile imitation of popular aesthetics or in the search for an ideal nation, and more in the permanent tension between—or juxtaposition of—modernity and backwardness, economy of means and stridency, elegance and 'bad taste'. This was a lesson learned with the *tropicalistas* and it reconfigured graphic design's discourse into a 'post-design design', to use Rafael Cardoso's provocation.

In a video made for the exhibition *From the Margin to the Edge*, which gathered thirty-three contemporary Brazilian artists in London, Rico Lins declared, 'I depart from the principle that attrition generates energy [...] Things that are not part of the same universe, when put together, create another context, a de-contextualisation'. Here we have a possible synthesis for the strength of Brazilian design at the beginning of the twenty-first century. The shock produced by the unexpected approximation of images, techniques, ideas and graphic material, creates a space that is less harmonious than the clichés of Brazilian culture might suggest, and one of the ways found to subvert these clichés was to focus on the least beautiful of the country's metropolises—São Paulo.

In the poster he created for the city, designer Gustavo Piqueira drew the silhouette of an old Kombi van, but stamped it with the Audi brand logo, in a cruel caricature of São Paulo's pretensions; in *O Livro Amarelo do Terminal*, a book project by Elaine Ramos and Maria Carolina Sampaio, the contents of one page leaks through to the other side, in a graphic suggestion of the movement of the crowds in the colossal São Paulo main bus station, the subject of the book.

The cover of *Pensar com Tipos* (Thinking with Type), a handbook on the most recent developments in digital typography by Ellen Lupton, was made using the rudimentary letterpress technique, typically used in the iconic *lambe-lambe* (wheat paste) posters that cover the walls of Brazilian cities. Thus, designer Elaine Ramos creates a technological juxtaposition, extracting text from the endless walls of São Paulo's peripheries and degraded downtown area, and placing it alongside digital type.

São Paulo—a metropolis of some 11 million inhabitants—was also the site of an inspired conceptual and visual experience: the 10th Architecture Biennale, which opened in 2013. Curated by Guilherme Wisnik, Ana Luiza Nobre and Ligia Nobre, the aim of the event was to occupy the city, bringing issues related to architecture and city planning to its streets, sidewalks, viaducts and even cemeteries. Design duo Daniel Trench and Celso Longo explored the polyphony and juxtaposition of discourses in the exhibition programme. In this project—arguably one of their best—typography was once again used to mime urban saturation through the use of all uppercase letters, the total occupation of empty spaces, and the use of the letter 'X' both as a number—to mark the 10th iteration of the biennale—and as an allusion to traffic cones and other objects related to urban construction. The colours—grey, white and yellow—further referenced the intention of turning the street into a theme, as did the chosen typeface, which looks stencilled like the letters used in asphalt signs. Each element possesses beauty, but still looks temporary.

In a city where visual design is so poor, this project by Longo and Trench opened up the possibility of providing São Paulo with high-quality design, attuned to the dirty and congested identity of the metropolis. It is also notable how, in an architecture exhibition, design has been able to affirm itself with such autonomy from an area with which, until recently, it maintained a relationship of dependency. Here, typography is not only the prevalent language, but also the sole language.

When we speak, therefore, of a tendency amongst the current generation of Brazilian designers to intensify contrasts and attritions, we are not speaking of a literal juxtaposition of images — so common in the digital age — but of a search for tension. When one incorporates, as an aesthetic and as a theme, the contrasts, the inequality, the obstacles to development and the violence in one's country, one also breaks with preconceived notions about one's culture.

An interesting example of this is the poster created by Rico Lins that went through three printing processes: typography, silkscreen and digital printing — random combinations of which ended up making each poster unique. 'I think serial reproduction is an interesting issue, but when you have no technological control over it, by creating a series of 500 posters in which each is different from the other, you play with the issues of serialization and of the unique piece of art,' Lins explained.

He looked to create 'layers of visual and graphic, as well as technological, space in such a way that, with very cheap, very popular technology, one can show this struggle of authorial graphic communication, fighting for the same piece of paper in the urban space'. In other words, Lins's poster was a representation of the marginal condition of graphic design in Brazil, squeezed between discourses on popular culture, which he said 'reflects the position of posters in Brazil, because this marginal condition brings with it a certain heroism, a possibility, an expressive freedom that other media do not have'.

Juxtaposition was also the technique chosen by the team that created the poster for the 28th São Paulo Art Biennial in 2008: Flávia Castanheira, Elaine Ramos and Daniel Trench used silkscreen to print an enormous red rectangle over the poster of the first São Paulo Art Biennial, an icon of modern art (and graphic arts) in the country since 1951. The original Modernist composition can be seen under the aggressive layer of bright, fluorescent ink — an ironic and corrosive interpretation of the history of the country's most important twentieth-century artistic institution, which was then facing a serious management and financial crisis.

From an aesthetic point of view, the most interesting experiments in contemporary Brazilian graphic design have been related to the most 'sacred' and conservative cultural object — the book — in the exact moment that it has been most challenged by new technologies. Over the past fifteen years, the traditional market reconfigured itself: album covers, which were perhaps the main showcase for Brazilian graphic design at the end of the twentieth century, lost their prominence due to the crisis in the music industry, and newspaper and magazine design faced successive setbacks that led to a huge increase of high-circulation publications.

At the same time, the apocalyptic prophecies about the end of book publishing could already be heard, but this countdown to the 'end' of printed materials and its inevitable digitalization ended up providing a stimulus for investigating the possibilities of paper, as if they had not been exhausted after all. Designer and historian Chico Homem de Melo saw this as a leap from a bi-dimensional universe to a full conquest of tri-dimensionality and of the potential poetic meanings of each element of each object. Thus, designers are no longer limited to conceiving the front and back covers of the book, but can also choose the paper, the format and the printing techniques in order to produce a complete tactile experience.

Such a change in direction, at the height of digital culture, under the empire of photography and Photoshop, represents a questioning of new technologies through traditional graphic techniques. Curiously, it was the generation born in a totally digital world that guaranteed the 'artistic' survival of movable type, silkscreen, photocopying, Letraset, cordel engravings and other archaic or artisanal printing techniques whose poetic value has been rediscovered.

This interest in popular, less rationalistic techniques is part of a wider concern, of uniting modern design with a hypothetical national identity. Just as in Mexico and other Latin American countries, the attempt to incorporate elements of the popular visual repertoire was constant in the 1990s, when the possibilities of digital technology still fascinated everyone. The *lambe-lambe* used on the cover of the typography book or the Rico Lins poster is not merely a reference — that is, it is not photographed, digitalized and transformed into a digital type — it is printed directly onto the object. Rudimentary, it highlights the 'flaws' that make each copy unique. Design, here, becomes literally 'graphic', as the material conditions of its production determine its result.

There is another aspect of Brazilian design that deserves attention in the first decades of the twenty-first century. From the start of the new millennium, an editorial boom allowed the design output of previous decades to be organized, systematized, debated and then published. At the same time, new cultural institutions have become labs for bold graphic design experiences. Chico Homem de Melo observes that, over the last fifteen years, design has also gained an academic relevance: many acclaimed designers also dedicate themselves to historical or theoretical research or to teaching, have organized books on the subject and studied the work of previous generations. In order to understand Brazilian design in the twenty-first century, one has to look at the production of the 1950s and 1960s.

This flurry of publications has allowed Brazilian production to circulate more freely both within Brazil and abroad: access to this 'forgotten treasure' of Brazilian graphic design, as New York Times design critic Steven Heller once described it, has rejuvenated the repertoire of new generations and projected the country's visual culture abroad. For the first time, a continuous line was traced synthesizing 200 years of graphic activity in the country, gathering materials unknown even to experts.

It is not just the subject matter of these titles that is worth exploring, their design is also often noteworthy: the rough and previously unknown path followed by Brazilian graphic design has been examined in detail in books such as *O Design Brasileiro Antes do Design*, by Rafael Cardoso, an award-winning 'metalinguistic' project designed by the art director of publishing company Cosac Naify, Elaine Ramos. Printed on paper traditionally used for making labels — matt on one side and glossy on the other — the jacket is made from pages from the book, randomly picked, folded and then labelled with the title and the author's name. 'In part, we have overvalued visual expression, in the sense that we used to make designs that were to be printed, but we ignored the material dimension of this print,' says Homem de Melo. 'Electronic design is more markedly visual. We no longer make graphic design, we make visual design. We have lost the dimension of matter, of volume...'

Monographs on the work of great Brazilian designers such as Alexandre Wollner, Rafic Farah and Bea Feitler put into circulation a repertoire that was much talked about, but not very well known. Rafael Cardoso, André Stolarski, Elaine Ramos and Chico Homem de Melo have all designed books that updated the library of available literature, which was woefully behind.

At the turn of the century, SESC-SP, a private institution established to carry out social welfare programmes and host cultural events, became a new nucleus for the promotion of Brazilian design. 'At SESC, I have a level of dialogue, of openness, that I cannot find anywhere else', said Homem de Melo. SESC has become an important and bold client, something particularly unique in a country where visual communication is hardly seen as a necessity. When it promotes festivals such as Videobrasil and contemporary art shows, musical festivals and other events in its busy cultural programme, it places great importance on graphic design — just as it has with architecture since the 1980s, sponsoring bold initiatives such as SESC Pompeia, a culture and sports centre designed by Lina Bo Bardi, and now one of the main references of São Paulo's Modernist architecture.

There is no doubt that typography is the favourite bet for a majority of the new generation of Brazilian designers, such as the ones we have mentioned, often reflecting a stubbornness, a profession of faith in 'pure' graphic design, and frequently, a denial of photography or the most literal forms of representation. Although voluminous, this production is certainly restricted to a more sophisticated section of the market, and although it is produced on an industrial scale it still has not penetrated Brazilian mass culture. In a sense, it only works one way: mass culture, in a typically *tropicalista* gesture, inoculates erudite culture, but the opposite is not yet true.

The steady performance of the Brazilian economy since the stabilization of the currency in 1994 has enabled the development of cultural projects that brought back into circulation important works of art and photographic collections. Large exhibitions such as the *Mostra do Redescobrimento* (The Re-Discovery Exhibition), the digitalization of historical collections, and the restoration by private institutions such as the Instituto Moreira Salles of important photography collections, have allowed for a reassessment of the Modern heritage and a new appreciation of Brazilian art and design.

One of the immediate consequences of this re-appreciation was the sudden adoption of an alternative to the excessive use of stock photos, often by anonymous artists — a phenomenon that took hold in the first years of digital photography, aided by the 'infinite' possibilities of the internet. The designers that managed to resist the temptations of stock picture libraries and turned their attention to the national visual repertoire, until then unknown to the public and to themselves, obtained interesting results, particularly for the formation of a 'Brazilian' graphic design aesthetic. The exploration and management of this 'new' source of material brought a national anchor to an increasingly internationalized activity. For young graphic designers, this meant direct access to a visual history that had often seemed locked, unattainable or restricted; for some of the more established designers, it was an opportunity to carry out ambitious projects, with unpublished or virtually unknown raw materials. In both cases, the results have been truly exciting and distinctly Brazilian.

Daniel Trench & Celso Longo

Daniel Trench and Celso Longo have worked together since 2007 and developed a number of significant projects — including books, catalogues and exhibition designs — for SESC-SP, one of the largest patrons of graphic design in Brazil. As with many of their colleagues at the AGI, they are particularly interested in the investigation of obsolete printing techniques and processes, which emphasize the graphic nature of design, such as photo-copying and screen printing. This is particularly evident in their visual identity for the 2013 exhibition *Mais de Mil Brinquedos Para a Criança Brasileira* at SESC Pompeia which involved a multicolored isometric typeface silkscreened over cardboard.

Trench's academic background is in painting, having studied fine arts at the Fundação Armando Alvares Penteado (FAAP) and his work is clearly influenced by contemporary Brazilian art. Longo, on the other hand, graduated in architecture from FAU-USP. Although they still complete solo projects, the majority of their work is now collaborative and they tend to focus their efforts on cultural programmes. 'I believe our work is very sharp. I like to think that each project has a core issue that needs to be handled and resolved. The challenge is to find the best solution without beating around the bush, going head on', says Longo. Both are also professors for the visual design programme at ESPM, in São Paulo.

Celso Longo: born São Paulo, 1977
Daniel Trench: born São Paulo, 1978

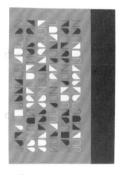 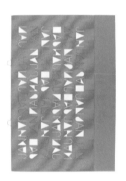  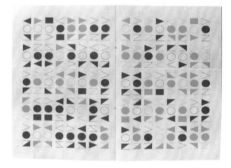

1.

  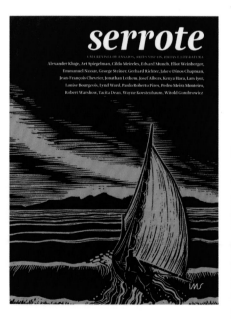

2.

1.
Visual identity for
SESC Pompeia offices,
2013

2.
Serrote magazine,
2009—13

3.
Quadrienal de Praga,
2011

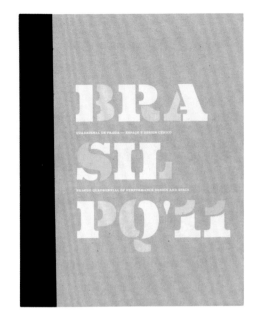

3.

4.

Na sua edição nº 3, *serrote* publicou a clássica série de fotos que Walker Evans fez no metrô de Nova York. No verão de 2009, Jorge Colombo, artista português radicado em Nova York (veja a "Carta dos editores", p. 3), participou da coletiva *Summer Readers*, da Jen Bekman Gallery. Os desenhos de Colombo, feitos a caneta sobre papel, flagram os passageiros do metrô em um momento único, o da leitura. Na sua semelhança, o gesto de ler aumenta a sensação de solidão e de mistério de cada viagem.

5.

6.

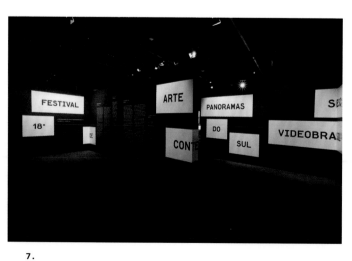

7.

8.

4.
Tutto Fellini, 2012

5.
Mostra SESC de Artes,
2008

6.
Serrote magazine,
2009-13

7-8.
18th Festival de Arte
Contemporânea SESC
Videobrasil, 2013

9.
Jazz na Fábrica, 2012

10.
Bienal de Arquitetura
de São Paulo logo, 2013

9.

10.

Elaine Ramos

Elaine Ramos's story is interlaced with that of the publishing company Cosac Naify, for whom she works as Art Director. She has helped coordinate their influential series of books about graphic design, transforming the publisher into one of the main centres of production and reflection on the subject in Brazil, and her style and vision has made their graphic identity one of the most coherent and refreshing in the Brazilian editorial market.

Ramos graduated from the Faculdade de Arquitetura e Urbanismo at the University of São Paulo (FAU-USP). Belonging to the generation that grew up during the cultural and political renewal following the end of Brazil's dictatorship, she assimilated in her work both *tropicalista* influences, visible in pieces such as the *Coleção Moda Brasileira*, and certain Modernist principles, which had previously been reduced to stale dogmas.

The result is a series of projects with a rare mix of sobriety and experimentation. Her generation is one of the first to work fully in the digital era, but which also dedicated itself to the investigation of materials and forms, as well as obsolete printing techniques. The *Coleção Particular* (Private Collection), which revisits literary classics, is an example of how Ramos balances the industrial demands of a publishing business with the creativity of an artist's book, artisanal and experimental.

A member of the Brazilian team at the Alliance Graphique Internationale (AGI), Ramos has earned numerous international awards, such as AIGA's 50 Books/50 Covers prize, for *O Livro Amarelo do Terminal*.

Born in São Paulo, 1974

1.
'Zazie no Metrô' book design, 2010

2.
'Linha do Tempo do Design Gráfico no Brasil' book design, 2012

3—4.
'Coleção Moda Brasileira' book design, 2010

1.

2.

3.

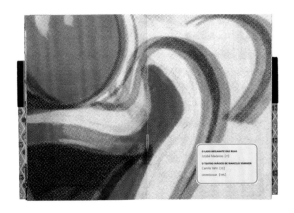

4.

Yomar Augusto

Yomar Augusto is a typographic artist and graphic designer, currently based in New York City. He initially trained in graphic design before going on to study photography at the School of Visual Arts in New York City in 2001, and later completing a Masters degree in type design at the Royal Academy of Art in The Hague, The Netherlands. This varied creative education clearly informs his current work, which often includes elaborate, calligraphic typefaces.

Custom type is inherent in both his client-based design and self-initiated art projects—in 2009–10 Augusto designed the rounded monolinear typeface Unity as the official typeface for Adidas during the 2010 FIFA World Cup in South Africa. Initially intended just for the strip, the typeface expanded to become an integral component of a comprehensive campaign and was applied to all Adidas screen, print and film components during the World Cup as well as the shirts of the Argentinian, Mexican, French, Danish and German national teams.

Augusto has presented both commercial and conceptual projects at solo exhibitions in Japan, Europe and Brazil and designed for a host of brands such as EMI, MTV & Warner music in Brazil, 180 Amsterdam and Random House in New York. He taught an advertising typography course at the Willem de Kooning Academy in Rotterdam between 2011 and 2012 and at the Bauhaus University in Weimar, Germany. He has also held experimental calligraphy and book art workshops in many countries, including Brazil, USA, Russia, Turkey, China, Denmark and Spain

Born in Brasília, 1977

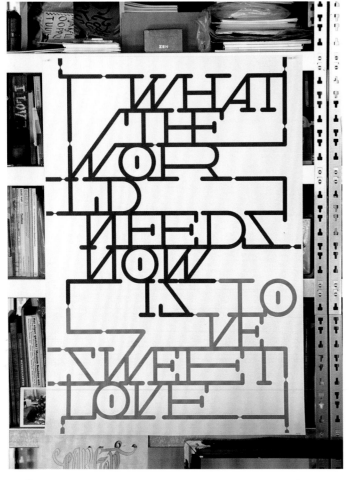

1.

2.

1.
Nick Bell poster, 2011

2.
Type textile, 2011

3.
More is More, 2012

4–5.
Martha Graham concept
and typography, 2012

3.

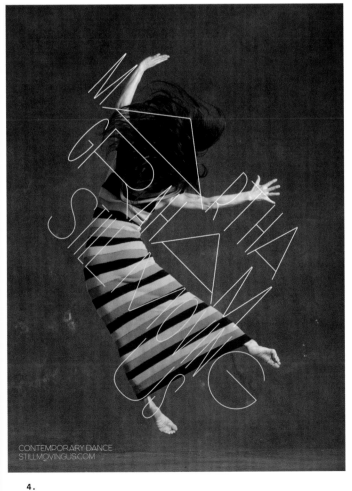

4.

5.

Kiko Farkas

Kiko Farkas graduated in architecture from the University of São Paulo (USP), and belongs to the generation of creatives that began their careers in the 1980s, when the teaching and practice of design were still in their early stages in Brazil. At the time, the country's only industrial design courses were based in Rio de Janeiro; people such as Farkas in São Paulo were forced to study architecture instead.

His visual repertoire is undoubtedly informed by his creative upbringing: son of Hungarian-Brazilian Thomaz Farkas (1924–2011), one of the biggest names in twentieth-century Brazilian photography, Farkas reconciled the Modernist legacy with the strident visuality of *tropicalismo* that had influenced Brazilian culture since the end of the 1960s. He also had access to international references at a time when Brazilian design was still very much introverted—while still young, he discovered cutting-edge European design through his father's collection of magazines.

His office, Máquina Estúdio, founded in 1987, is one of the main centres of editorial design in Brazil, and its work is renowned for its rigorous and elegant construction and palette of vivid colours, which clearly show the *tropicalista* influence. There is something distinctly retro about his curved forms and sober use of typography. Amongst his most interesting work is the series of posters created from 2003 to 2007 for the São Paulo Orquestra do Estado (OSESP), in which he experimented with the random serialization and recombination of elements in a highly graphic approach.

Born in São Paulo, 1957

1.

2.

3.

4.

5.

FUNDAÇÃO
THEATRO
MUNICIPAL DE
SÃO PAULO
TEMPORADA
2014

CORAL
PAULISTANO
MÁRIO
DE ANDRADE

THEATRO
MUNICIPAL DE
SÃO PAULO
TEMPORADA
2014

CORAL
PAULISTANO
MÁRIO
DE ANDRADE

1.

ORQUESTRA
EXPERIMENTAL DE
REPERTÓRIO
CICLO DAS
SINFONIAS DE
BEETHOVEN

PRAÇA
DAS
ARTES
TEMPORADA
2014

1.
Coleçao Poesias/Poetry
Collection, 2011–14

2.
Poster for the OSESP,
2004

3–6.
Posters for the Theatro
Municipal de São Paulo,
2014

Rico Lins

Born in 1955, Rico Lins completed, through his studies and celebrated professional career, the cycle which took Brazilian design from Modernist purism to the noisy plurality we see at the start of the twenty-first century. His tremendous ability to guide younger professionals has made him a mentor for many designers and an important reference for students. The oldest Brazilian member of the Alliance Graphique Internationale (AGI), Lins has always championed the entry of new members, as well as the realization of the AGI Open congress in São Paulo in 2014.

Lins graduated in 1979 from Brazil's temple of design, ESDI-Rio — the institution responsible for the generation of designers that introduced many of the rigorous graphic design principles that are taken for granted today. From the start, his work revealed the aesthetic and political trademarks of the tumultuous 1970s and 1980s in a Brazil under military dictatorship.

During his lengthy stays in France, the United Kingdom and the United States, Lins promoted dialogue with the international scene and helped broaden the horizon for Brazilian design references.

Lins seeks the re-approximation of design and the graphic arts. Much of his prize-winning work uses multiple techniques, such as the poster series *Seja Marginal* (Be Marginal), which mixes the primitive letterpress of São Paulo's street posters with both screen printing and offset printing.

He has won many design awards, including gold medals from the NY Art Directors Club and the Society of Publication Designers, the 2001 Design by Designers award and the Merit Award of the Type Directors Club, in 2007. He has been a member of AGI since 1997.

Born in Rio de Janeiro, 1955

1.

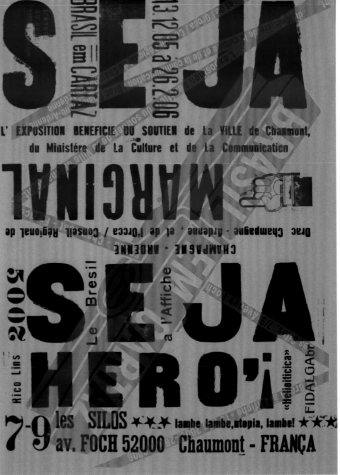

2.

1.
Kultur Revolution,
1982-2008

2.
Brasil em Cartaz, 2005

3.
Zoomp, 1997-98

4.
Panamericana 96, 1996

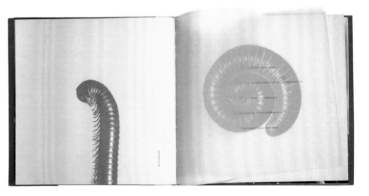

3.

4.

Arnaldo Antunes

Criolo

Racionais MC's

Claudia Leitte

Caetano Veloso

Gal Costa

Clarice Falcão

Marisa Monte

Paulo Terron

music

It's very hard to define what Brazil sounds like—unsurprising, perhaps, for a country with a surface area of more than 8.5 million km² (3.3 million square miles) and almost 200 million inhabitants. It is a country that has fostered many musical styles, and all of them have produced hits. Even the internationally-renowned *Música popular Brasileira* (Brazilian popular music) or MPB is really just a label attributed to the artists whose music does not fit clearly into any one style. That said, it is certainly extremely popular: a recent survey by the Instituto Brasileiro de Opinião Pública e Pesquisa—IBOPE (Brazilian Institute of Research and Public Opinion) revealed that after *sertanejo*—the Brazilian country-style music—MPB is the second most cited musical style by listeners in the main Brazilian capitals, being mentioned by 47 per cent of respondents.

At the turn of the twenty-first century, the musical world drastically changed: the recording industry fell victim to online piracy all over the world, but in Brazil the widespread sale of unauthorized copies on the streets made matters even worse. In 2011, when the industry was actually celebrating a slight market reaction, the Cinema and Music Antipiracy Association (APCM) estimated that illegal copies represented 48–65 per cent of the market—putting Brazil among the ten largest consumers of musical piracy in the world.

This change in the status quo—when record labels stopped being the main distributors and advertisers of music—had a knock-on effect on the creative output of the industry: new talents emerged, fighting for space, and the established names had to rethink strategies to maintain financial viability in this new and unfamiliar post-Internet world. 'I once went to a large record label and they told me: "If you had come here ten years ago, we would have put a big bag of money in front of you"', recalls singer Tulipa Ruiz, who released her debut album, *Efêmera*, in 2010. 'Once, those amounts were common, but no more…'

The daughter of Luiz Chagas—who played electric guitar for singer-songwriter Itamar Assumpção in the 1980s—Tulipa started out singing informally in bars before deciding to embark on a musical career. She has never depended on the industry; the experience has always been an entirely independent effort. 'When I started working on my first record I already had a team: production, PR, I pressed the record myself.' Later, when it came to organizing live shows, the singer tried to adapt to the old school model, but she soon realized that the record labels' structure was not adapted to the new era. 'I thought I should look for help in the industry,' she explains. 'We went to a few labels, had many meetings. Nothing that they suggested fitted with my model—I already had what they were offering. I distributed and advertised my work myself. The model was too outdated, and the percentages were unfair. It did not fit into what I was doing, so I kept going with my pilot project, and, little by little, I structured myself.'

In a similar manner, *Paulistano* rapper Emicida made headlines in 2009 when he independently produced and distributed more than 3,000 copies of the mixtape *Pra Quem Já Mordeu Um Cachorro Por Comida, Até Que Eu Cheguei Longe* (For a Guy Who Once Bit A Dog For Food, I've Come A Long Way). The strategy could not have been simpler: he recorded the CD himself—at home—and then sold it at concerts and in stores. Each unit cost him around R$1 (£0.26) to produce and he sold it for anything from R$2 (£0.52) upwards. 'My minimum profit is R$1, but many people spontaneously pay more than R$2,' he told *Época* magazine at the time. 'They say it is worth more and pay up to R$20.' The rapper used the same strategy for subsequent records and says he has sold more than 30,000 units, counting everything he released before his first complete album, the independent *O Glorioso Retorno de Quem Nunca*

Esteve Aqui (The Glorious Return of He Who Was Never Here, 2013). For Tulipa, this direct contact with an audience is so important for new artists. 'Today, we count on an interested public. You have to count on this public to disseminate [your work].' For her, the structure works extremely well: some even say that her records sell more than the most recent releases from icon Caetano Veloso, who has a contract with Universal.

Blockbuster hits, however, are still reserved for acts driven by the TV networks—especially Globo—and also for the religious music market. In 2012, the bestsellers in Brazil were country singer Paula Fernandes, whose live album *Paula Fernandes: Ao Vivo* sold more than 1.3 million copies, catholic priest Marcelo Rossi, who sold 1.2 million copies of his *Ágape Musical* and gospel singer Aline Barros with *Extraordinário Amor de Deus* (Extraordinary Love of God) selling 392,000 copies. All three artists have contracts with recording labels, proving that in Brazil, music is consumed in more than one way. While the mainstream, mass-consumption market still exists, another more specific path can be taken by independent artists, because there is room for them too. 'Fifteen years ago the percentages offered by record labels were worthwhile [for smaller artists] because they used to sell a lot of records,' says Tulipa Ruiz, 'you ended up making a lot of money. But today the percentage is the same, and one does not sell much. The artist's percentage becomes dismal'.

A rare case of these two worlds overlapping can be seen in the example of Banda Calypso, a musical duo from Pará. It is estimated that the band has sold between 12 and 15 million records, but there are no official records, as although it has had various contracts with labels in the past, Calypso is an independent band that sells its own work. 'If we had launched the album with a record label, it would not have done so well, because they had artists who were higher priorities—they would not work so hard on ours', said the band's guitarist Chimbinha to *Trip* magazine, referring to their first album, *Volume 1* (1999). Calypso's market was initially restricted to the state of Pará, which is virtually autonomous due to its geographical location in the north, far from the Rio-São Paulo axis and known for the local musical style *tecno brega*—a cheesy brand of techno music that reworks and remixes popular music, especially from the 1980s, which has recently become hugely popular in the area. Chimbinha explains how they decided to set out independently: 'It was an idea generated by necessity. I did not stop to think about [the independent distribution system], I just did it. Since we did not have a label, we did our own distribution in the beginning. Joelma [the lead singer] was on the phone, writing down the orders. I went to the post office and sent the albums all over Brazil. That is how it started'.

Whether selling 30,000 home-pressed CDs or 15 million through a record label, one thing is clear: new Brazilian artists cannot be afraid of challenging the norm. 'When I made my album available for free on the Internet, it stayed for a few weeks among the best sellers in stores,' says Tulipa. 'Free downloads increased physical sales.' For her, this feared enemy of the musical industry is not necessarily negative. It is something that can actually help musicians gain more control over their work, selecting the experience that listeners will have. 'It's more well rounded. The person can assess you by listening to your work in decent quality—not a draft of my song that they hear on YouTube or in a bad-quality MP3. I prefer that they listen to the whole product, the complete package.'

Criolo, an artist from São Paulo, also realized the potential of the internet. In 2011, he made his album *Nó na Orelha* (Knot in the Ear) available for free download. It quickly amassed thousands of fans with the melancholic ballad, 'Não Existe Amor em SP' (There's No Love in São Paulo) and the raps 'Subirusdoistiozin' and 'Grajauex'. The album—Criolo's second—was a milestone in his career: it was elected the best Brazilian album by *Rolling Stone Brasil* magazine, and was awarded three MTV Video Music Brasil awards (Album of the Year, Song of the Year for 'Não Existe Amor em SP' and Best New Artist). Criolo became a familiar face on television shows, performed concerts all over the country and also staged a number of international tours. 'It's so natural,' he says, talking of the distribution process in an interview with *Rolling Stone* magazine, 'there is no marketing strategy. For me, it is an honour to have it in long-play format, we have it [in this format] because we value the LP culture, and we will make it available on the Internet. It's that simple.'

The absence of a large record label behind the scenes does not mean that these new artists are left to fund everything themselves: in Brazil, fiscal incentive legislation such as Lei Rouanet (Rouanet Act, which guarantees fiscal exemption to businesses that support selected artists) and private grants help to launch careers. The extremely successful cosmetics company Natura is one such business involved in the Lei Rouanet, and enables artists such as multi-instrumentalist Marcelo Jeneci, to remain active. His debut album *Feito Pra Acabar* (Made to End), was recorded in 2010 with the help of the brand and then distributed by Som Livre, owned by Globo, which used songs like 'Amado' (Beloved) which was recorded with Vanessa da Mata, in the soundtracks of some of its TV shows. The process was repeated with *De Graça* (For Free, 2013), which the public could listen to online for free before it was sold physically in stores.

In recent years Brazil has seen the emergence of several new distribution platforms such as a local iTunes Store and streaming services Deezer, Spotify and Rdio, highlighting Brazil's evolving future. Another great force in this evolution is the constant expansion of the mobile phone market: it is estimated that, by 2016, the number of smartphones in the country will have grown from 12.6 million to 33 million. Sixth in the world in terms of production of and audience for YouTube videos (according to *Billboard* magazine), Brazil's digital music distribution seems destined to change in the next few years.

Before the mid-1990s, it would have been unthinkable for big names such as Maria Bethânia and Chico Buarque to record their work with small, independent labels. The Brazilian market was simply not used to this format and all artists sat comfortably in the laps of large corporations. Rio-based record company Biscoito Fino, which opened in 1993, was the first independent organization to emerge and buck this trend, and today both artists are signed to the label.

'The expected sales of a new album are much less than they used to be,' said Buarque to *Rolling Stone Brasil* magazine in 2011, on the release of *Chico*, his second album with Biscoito Fino. 'So I tried to compensate the label for its investment, contributing to their release project, on the Internet and so on. But this is not my business.' For him, literature, his second, and also very successful, occupation, guarantees part of his income. Today, Chico rigorously alternates between releasing records and books. 'The books actually sell more than the albums,' he says, 'and the books are sold abroad too. I don't worry about it.' Buarque sees the alternation between one form of art and the other as a part of his current creative process—something that is independent of distribution strategies and even of the musical industry as a whole. Between 1966 and 1989, he released close to thirty studio albums, including movie soundtracks and works in Spanish and Italian. Between 1990 and 2013, he released only seven. 'What happens is that, today, composing

1.

has become such a rare act that, every time I write a song, I remember it exactly — I know the history of each composition, because it is a special moment,' he explains. 'It is normal for every composer, for every creator, to lose that youthful enthusiasm [as time goes by], that whole creative exuberance. He becomes a more selective creator.'

In the case of more prolific artists such as Maria Bethânia, a smaller label means virtually unrestricted artistic freedom. The singer has her own sub-label within Biscoito Fino — Quitanda — through which she releases up to two studio albums per year. Between 2002 and 2013 she launched thirteen albums, including a couple of live records. 'I like the rehearsals the most — I like them more than concerts. Quitanda is like a rehearsal, with the option of making mistakes... of making discoveries,' Bethânia told *IstoÉ* magazine in 2003. With her label, she doesn't need to worry so much about financial concerns (in Quitanda, the production costs are shared between the label and the singer). 'I don't like wondering if I am going to sell a million or a hundred albums — I am terrible at this. I am very coy, needy, insecure — like anyone who deals with public exposure. At Biscoito Fino I am cared for.'

While some artists have had to adapt to new forms of distribution, others have decided to change their style. Caetano Veloso, possibly the best known Brazilian musician currently recording, took a drastic change in direction in 2006 with the release of *Cê* (which took its title from the colloquial Portuguese word for 'you'). After years working with musical director Jaques Morelembaum, who composed some remarkable (but conservative) arrangements for records such as *Fina Estampa* (Fine Print, 1994) and *Noites do Norte* (Northern Nights, 2000), the singer and songwriter from Bahia created Banda Cê, formed by young musicians from the Rio rock scene. 'I composed [the songs] thinking about the instruments', Veloso said in an interview with *Bizz* magazine on the album's release. 'I took with me, in my guitar, insinuations of everything that I wanted to happen in the instruments. There is a sense of composing and treating songs as a band would do, and I really like it that the work method is that of a band — but we are not one. It's not like we had been working together for a long time.'

Veloso kept recording and performing in concerts with this classic rock band formation — electric guitars, bass and drums — with praise from critics and a renewed audience. The experience encouraged him to think about what he could do to inject some of that energy into his fellow artists. The strategy worked surprisingly well for Gal Costa — a singer who recorded *Domingo* (Sunday, 1967), the first album of her career with Veloso and has collaborated with him ever since. Costa had previously released a series of thematic projects, including Bossa Nova albums and Tom Jobim tributes, but the new project with Veloso — *Recanto* (2011) — injected a dose of rock as well as elements of electronic music. During the first performance in Rio de Janeiro of the album (which was fully composed by Veloso for Costa), the shock generated by the singer's change in musical direction was clear — during one of the songs, a lady that shared a table with Veloso enquired 'Is it supposed to sound like this?' (thinking it must have been a result of a malfunction in the sound system) before an annoyed Veloso replied, 'this is contemporary electronic music!'

For Marisa Monte, Carlinhos Brown and Arnaldo Antunes it was not necessary to change musical direction; it made more sense to combine their existing styles. The trio — all three with respected solo careers — decided to unite in 2001. They rehearsed for two days and spent the next thirteen days recording one song per day, all new. The album was self-titled with the name that the group chose for itself — Tribalistas — and was released in

2002. They were notoriously averse to publicity, refusing to give interviews about the project and avoiding live performances. The only explanation seemingly came from the lyrics of the song 'Tribalistas' which stated: 'O Tribalismo é um antimovimento / Que vai se desintegrar no próximo momento' (Tribalism is an anti-movement / Which will disintegrate in the next moment). The profusion of different rhythms that permeated the album's songs was something that many critics saw as a revision of what *tropicalismo* had done decades earlier.

The band's popularity was immediate and far-reaching: tracks 'Velha Infância', 'É Você' and 'Já Sei Namorar' were constantly played on Brazilian radio stations and the latter was released as a single in European countries such as Italy, France and Holland with moderate success. In Portugal, it was a chart-topper. It was also nominated for Best Brazilian Song and Record of the Year at the 2003 Latin Grammy Awards. It sold more than 1.5 million copies in Brazil.

Just as suddenly as they appeared on the scene, Tribalistas vanished. The trio performed live during the Latin Grammy Awards ceremony in 2003 (although the concert was not broadcast in its entirety), briefly reunited during a Marisa Monte concert to launch the Brazilian iTunes platform in 2011 and, during the peak of the public debate on gay marriage in Brazil, made their track 'Joga Arroz' available for free download, but curiously it was individually credited to Marisa Monte, Carlinhos Brown and Arnaldo Antunes.

Even amidst the fickleness of the contemporary Brazilian music scene, there are some genres that remain consistently popular. *Sertanejo*, for example, is the style of music that has produced the most sales over the last few years, and according to the 2013 IBOPE survey is the most popular in Brazil, with more than half of the respondents stating it as their favourite type of music. In the second half of the 1980s, this evolution of Brazilian country music exploded throughout Brazil, with duos such as Chitãzinho & Xororó, Zezé Di Camargo & Luciano and Leandro & Leonardo dominating the market. At the start of the twenty-first century *sertanejo* gained force when it was rebranded as 'university *sertane*' (giving it a more youthful air) or 'roots music' (a classification that implied a certain credibility, since it denotes a connection to the style's origins).

It is not surprising, therefore, that *sertanejo* is the main export of Brazilian music, mainly thanks to Michel Teló from Paraná, and his song 'Ai Se Eu Te Pego' (If I Catch You) released in 2011. The catchy track — a mixture of electronic instruments and an accordion — became an international hit even though it is sung in Portuguese (an English version was later released, with limited success). The song featured in the music charts across Europe and North America from Hungary to Mexico and reportedly reached 7.2 million purchased downloads. Teló opened up the international market for other musicians, such as Gusttavo Lima, whose single 'Balada' in 2012 was almost as successful.

Ivete Sangalo, a singer from Bahia of *axé* music, a movement that emerged in the Carnival street blocks of Salvador that fuses different Afro-Caribbean genres such as marcha, reggae and calypso, is also a constant presence in the best-seller lists. It is estimated that, between her solo career and records released when she was the lead singer for Banda Eva, she has sold more than 20 million albums. Ivete has also been nominated twenty times for the Latin Grammy, having won two awards. The natural path for her was to break on to the international scene — something she acheived in 2010 with the live album *Ivete Sangalo ao Vivo no Madison Square Garden*, recorded at the famous New York arena, featuring collaborations with Canadian singer Nelly Furtado, Argentinian Diego Torres and Colombian artist Juanes. In a review by Jon Pareles, *The New York Times* noted that her international strategy needed some adjustment. 'She tried one international crossover strategy: putting synthesizers and a common-denominator 4/4 club beat under one medley of hits. But completely giving up that Brazilian propulsion would neutralize her music. It's the crossover dilemma, and one that Ms. Sangalo still needs to work out.'

With a 50-year-strong career, if there is someone who does not fail to surprise with the size of his commercial successes, it is Roberto Carlos. 'I don't know any other artist who is able to release a new hit of such magnitude', said Brazilian Sony Music's CEO, Alexandre Schiavo, when assessing the success of the song 'Esse Cara Sou Eu', launched in 2012, in an interview with *Rolling Stone Brasil* magazine. 'It surprised everyone because the format in which it was released has no history.' The format rescued from limbo by the musician was EP, which had disappeared from the Brazilian market years before. In about a month, the 4-track CD sold more than 1.3 million copies. This potential remains unexploited: the latest studio album by Roberto Carlos, *Roberto Carlos,* was released in 2005. After this, the singer launched six live albums, many of them thematic: *Duetos* (2006, featuring duets) and *En Vivo* (with songs in Spanish), among others.

A similar 'active inactivity' strategy has been adopted by rock band Los Hermanos. Officially, the quartet had gone into an 'indefinite hiatus' in April 2007, two years after their last studio album, *4*. After that, there were three reunions for live performances: in 2009, when they opened Radiohead's Brazilian tour concerts; in 2010, for SWU festival, which was preceded by some concerts in the northeast of Brazil; and in a large national tour in 2012, with 12 concerts celebrating their fifteen-year anniversary. 'This is not a structured process, that is, each of these encounters happened without an appointment for the next time', explained keyboardist Bruno Medina to *Rolling Stone Brasil* in 2012. 'This is how it's been, with no great expectations.' In this last reunion, Los Hermanos sold 15,000 tickets in ten hours for the Rio de Janeiro concerts and in São Paulo, they sold 16,000 in twenty-four hours. For Medina, the success can at least be partly credited to the public's renewed interest. 'The most important legacy of this period [of Los Hermanos' existence], in my opinion, is to realize that there are sixteen and seventeen-year olds discovering our music now, anxious to see the band live for the first time.'

As Caetano Veloso argues, 'MPB' is an unfair label, especially because it is so limiting in the face of Brazilian music's variety. There are many approaches to analyzing music produced domestically: classifying it by region, by the way in which it is consumed and, occasionally, by the impact it has abroad. Yet, it is actually the lack of general limiting characteristics that makes Brazilian music so exciting.

2.
Caetano Veloso live in
São Paulo, 2013

2.

Arnaldo Antunes

Arnaldo Antunes first took to the musical stage as a member of the rock group Titãs, in the early 1980s. In its classic formation, the band had eight members—a rather unusual format, but one that was to prove successful. Titãs released countless hits over the years, and reinvented its musical style many times, most radically with their third album, the aggressive *Cabeça Dinossauro* (1986), which included six singles released into the charts, half of them written or co-written by Antunes.

Antunes's talent for songwriting sent him down two different paths: composing songs for popular artists such as Marisa Monte ('Beija Eu' and 'Infinito Particular' amongst others) and an acclaimed career as a poet, publishing more than a dozen books including *As Coisas* (1992) and *Animais* (2011).

When he left Titãs in the early 1990s, Antunes kept on writing songs for his former bandmates and occasionally joined them for concerts and recordings, but mainly focussed on his solo career. Between 1993 and 2014, Arnaldo Antunes released ten studio albums, three live recordings and three collaborative projects: Tribalistas (with Marisa Monte and Carlinhos Brown), *Pequeno Cidadão* (with music for kids) and *A Curva da Cintura* (with Edgard Scandurra and Toumani Diabaté, from Mali).

Born in São Paulo, 1960

1.

2.

3.

1.
'Disco' album cover,
2013

2.
'Iê Iê Iê' album cover,
2009

3.
Arnaldo Antunes, 2013

Criolo

Kleber Gomes discovered the world of rhymes when he was still a child in Grajaú, a neighbourhood in the far south of São Paulo. Later, in the mid-2000's, having adopted the pen name Criolo Doido, he founded an itinerant event called the Rinha dos MCs (or battle of MCs) — a mixture between a ball, rapper battles, DJ performances and a street art exhibition. He also released the album *Ainda Há Tempo* (2006) and the DVD *Live in SP* (2010), both essentially focused on rap. But, in 2011, the artist's sound changed direction.

Accompanied by producer and musician Daniel Ganjaman, he dropped the 'Doido' from his name and recorded *Nó na Orelha*, which was distributed for free on the internet. The rhymes were not abandoned, but they were accompanied by band arrangements from Ganjaman, who also introduced Criolo to a more melodic style of singing. The melancholy, disillusioned single 'Não Existe Amor em SP' was the first to extrapolate the world of hip-hop, becoming an online viral phenomenon.

The album was elected as the best of the year by critics at *Rolling Stone Brasil* magazine, and Criolo went on a lengthy tour around Brazil. He also played in Europe, once in a duet with legendary Ethiopian musician Mulatu Astatke. In 2013, he released the DVD *Criolo & Emicida Ao Vivo*, together with another representative of São Paulo's contemporary rap scene, Emicida.

Born in São Paulo, 1975

1.

2.

3.

1.
'Duas de Cinco' single
cover, 2013

2.
'Subirusdoistiozin'
LP cover, 2010

3.
Criolo live on stage,
2013

Racionais MC's

Racionais MC's are a unique case on the Brazilian musical scene. The rap quartet — formed by MCs Mano Brown, Ice Blue and Edi Rock with DJ KL Jay — managed to gain nationwide popularity without ever having been signed to a large record company or performing on a TV show for Globo, Brazil's largest broadcaster.

All the band's hits — which they have released consistently for almost a quarter of a century — have been more or less spontaneous, without a big marketing plan to support them. The musicians' focus was always the social message that they transmitted, not entertainment in itself.

Even when the video for 'Sobrevivendo no Inferno', a raw, straightforward song about the massacre of more than one hundred prisoners in a São Paulo detention centre in 1992, won MTV Brazil's most prestigious award in 1998, Racionais did not change course.

The effort and focus on the message paid off. 'Rap changed many things', said Ice Blue, years later, in an interview to *Rolling Stone Brasil* magazine. 'It taught people not to be ashamed of where they live, of their hair, of their skin colour, and enabled them to speak about their lives.' Today, the group is preparing a much-anticipated new album, the first one since *Nada Como Um Dia Após o Outro Dia* (2002), and the members divide their time between concerts and their own solo careers.

Formed in São Paulo, 1988

1.

2.

3.

1.
Racionais MC's, 2012

2.
Mano Brown, 2012

3.
Racionais MC's live on stage, 2013

Claudia Leitte

Born in Rio de Janeiro, but with a soul from Bahia, Claudia Leitte began her musical career singing in the bars of Salvador, gaining national attention when she joined *axé* music band Babado Novo. The band's frenetic approach to work generated five albums in seven years, and earned them hits such as 'Exttravasa' and 'Lirirrixa'.

She launched her solo career with the album *Ao Vivo em Copacabana* (2008), recorded during a concert on Rio's famous beach, but albums and DVDs are just a detail in Claudia's career, which revolves more around the energetic live performances that she gives in concerts and during Salvador's carnival block parties, always accompanied by thousands of fans.

In 2012 Leitte joined Carlinhos Brown, Lulu Santos and Daniel as a judge on 'The Voice Brasil', Globo's hit reality TV show. Riding on her wave of success, the singer released a new album, *Axemusic*, in 2014, at the beginning of the year in which Brazil will host the soccer World Cup—the official anthem of which, 'We Are One (Ole Ola)', Leitte sings alongside Latin superstars Pitbull and Jennifer Lopez.

Born in Rio de Janeiro, 1980

1.
Claudia Leitte live on stage, 2013

1.

Caetano Veloso

One of the most prolific of all Brazilian artists, Caetano Veloso, from Bahia, is also one of the most diverse, having experimented with many art forms from music and cinema to literature and theatre. A fan of bossa nova, and especially of João Gilberto's music, he started recording in the mid 1960s. His debut album, *Domingo* (1967) was recorded with musical partner Gal Costa.

Veloso's second album saw the emergence of *Tropicalismo* (or *Tropicália*, also the name of its opening song) — a movement he founded with Gilberto Gil, Tom Zé, Os Mutantes and others. It was then that Brazilian popular music became truly universal, using foreign instruments such as electric guitars — which produced a great aesthetic shock at the time. Persecuted by the military regime, Veloso and Gil went into exile. They lived in London from 1969 to 1972, a period in which Veloso recorded a number of his classic albums.

As a composer, Veloso explored countless Brazilian rhythms, from bossa nova to samba, including traditional carnival songs, *forró* and rock. Throughout the 1980s, 1990s and 2000s, he was consistently on the musical scene, going on tours and releasing close to thirty albums (including studio recordings, soundtracks, live albums and compilations). He won two Grammy awards (as well as nine Latin Grammy awards) and performed at the Academy Awards ceremony in 2003, singing 'Burn it Blue', nominated for Best Song, in a duet with Mexican singer Lila Downs.

Born in Santo Amaro, 1942

1.
Veloso live on stage at the Espaço das Américas, São Paulo, 2013

2.
Abraçaço album cover, 2012

1.

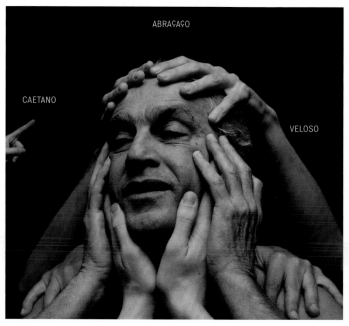

2.

Gal Costa

Gal Costa started her career alongside an impressively talented group—Caetano Veloso, Tom Zé, Maria Bethânia and Gilberto Gil—in the musical show 'Nós, Por Exemplo...' (1964) and she would continue to work with those artists from that day on. Her debut album, *Domingo* (1967), was recorded with Veloso and it clearly demonstrates their shared love of bossa nova. That same year, the artists from the show launched one of the largest movements in Brazilian music, *tropicalismo*.

The songs from this brilliant phase in Gal's career—with her potent voice at the service of Rogerio Duprat's arrangements and Lanny Gordin's electric guitar—can be heard in the collective albums *Tropicália ou Panis Et Circenses* (1968), *Gal Costa* (1969) and *Gal* (1969). But she reached her peak with the energetic live album

Fa-Tal—Gal a Todo Vapor (1971), a recording of the 'Fatal' tour, directed by the poet Waly Salomão (co-author of 'Vapor Barato', one of Costa's greatest hits).

In the 1980s and 1990s, the singer maintained her position as an MPB giant—but she never lost her bold approach, apparent in her tour O Sorriso do Gato de Alice (1993), led by theatre director Gerald Thomas, in which she sang Cazuza's 'Brasil' baring her breasts. In 2012, in another partnership with Caetano Veloso, she launched 'Recanto', a successful foray into the world of contemporary music. This turnaround was received with enthusiasm by critics, who praised the album as a welcome breath of fresh air in Gal Costa's career.

Born in Salvador, 1945

1–2.
Gal Costa live on
stage, 2013

1.

2.

Clarice Falcão

An actress, screenwriter and singer, Clarice Falcão already had a solid television career when she became famous across the country as a member of comedy group Porta dos Fundos, which made its name producing online sketches. She was soon recognized for her musical talent, mixing clever lyrics with folksy rhythms directly influenced by bands such as Los Hermanos, as well as the more quirky British artist Kate Nash and American indie-pop group Magnetic Fields. In early 2013 Falcão rocketed to success in part due to her appearance in an advertising campaign for Brazilian supermarket chain Pão de Açúcar.

Her tracks are good-humoured, even comical, juxtaposing naiveté and absurdity, as in the unconventional love song 'Oitavo Andar' — in which she sweetly describes a murder/suicide, and the video for which has reached almost 5 million views online. When asked if she thought listeners would confuse her songs with her comedic career, Falcão replied, 'I hope not. The joke lasts less time than the music. A joke told ten times loses grace; a song heard ten times, not necessarily [...] What I wanted to do was make arrangements with the most beautiful music as music, regardless of the joke'.

Her songs were compiled in a self-titled EP in 2013, followed by a complete album, *Monomania*. The same year, the singer was nominated in the Best New Artist category at the Latin Grammy Awards.

Born in Recife, 1989

1.
Clarice Falcão live on stage, Belo Horizonte, 2013

1.

Marisa Monte

When Marisa Monte released her first album *MM* in 1989, she was already an accomplished singer, having studied operatic singing and *bel canto* since she was fourteen years old, even spending some time in Italy to improve her skills. But it was this album's popular style — with songs such as 'Comida', 'Chocolate' and 'O Xote das Meninas' — that really helped her find her path. Half a million copies were sold, and a new MPB star was born.

Monte's musical sophistication, allied with a globally-appealing repertoire, helped drive her career, which gradually became more authorial. For the album *Mais* (1991), she wrote (or co-wrote) five of the twelve tracks, including the hit 'Beija Eu'. From that moment on, her popularity soared — *Memórias, Crônicas e Declarações de Amor* (2000) inaugurated the Latin Grammy awards era: the song 'Amor I Love You' was nominated for Best Brazilian Song, and the album was the winner of the Best Brazilian Contemporary Pop Album category.

After a collaboration project with Carlinhos Brown and Arnaldo Antunes — the project Tribalistas, which released its only album in 2002 — Monte simultaneously launched two different works in 2006: 'Infinito Particular' and 'Universo ao Meu Redor'. Even with the crisis in the music industry, the artist has now sold well over 10 million albums. In the 2012 Olympics Closing Ceremony in London, she sang in the eight-minute hand-over that showcased Brazil, the event's next host.

Born in Rio de Janeiro, 1967

1.
Marisa Monte singing
live at the Congress
Palace in Madrid, 2013

1.

Cris Bierrenbach

Pedro Motta

Sofia Borges

Eustáquio Neves

Pio Figueiroa

Coletivo Garapa

João Castilho

Barbara Wagner

Rodrigo Braga

Odires Mlászho

Eder Chiodetto

photography

In February 1922, heavily influenced by the development of the first Brazilian metropolises, which were at that time enjoying an exuberance brought by the thriving coffee trade, a group of artists — mainly literary authors and painters — coordinated the São Paulo Modern Art Week. Two years later, poet Oswald de Andrade, one of the main organizers of the event, wrote the satirical essays *Manifesto Pau-Brasil* and *Manifesto Antropófago*. In a passage from the former, Andrade lists a number of concepts that would later fit perfectly into Brazilian experimental Modernist photography and the Concretist movement: 'Synthesis; Equilibrium; Invention; Surprise; A new perspective; A new scale...'

At that time Brazilian photography was still a long way from being affected by the conceptual and aesthetic ideas that vanguard artists were busy proposing in Europe. Photography did not feature in the Modern Art Week of 1922 as an artistic medium, but was simply used as a tool for documenting the event. The issues raised in Modernist movements such as Dadaism and Surrealism took nearly twenty-five years to filter down into Brazilian photographic production. The new perspective and scale urged by Andrade in his manifesto were finally approached at the end of the 1940s, primarily through the experiments of Geraldo de Barros, the main driver of the renewal of Brazilian photography during this period.

Trained in drawing and painting, as were most of his contemporaries, Barros at first dedicated himself to figurative painting, but after acquiring a Rolleiflex camera he began investigating the expressive possibilities of photography. In 1949, when Barros, who had studied in Europe for some time, joined the Foto Cine Clube Bandeirante — a group of photographers who worked together and participated in photography contests — he was shocked by the quality of the work he found there. The parameters used to judge images taken by club members were based on standards from academic painting mixed with a certain prosaic romanticism, and rather than shooting images of the dynamic mid-century Brazil developing outside their windows, the vogue inside the studio was for static imitations of still-life paintings.

Influenced by Gestalt theory — a branch of psychology that studies how individuals perceive elementary geometrical forms — Barros's photographic experiments, which play with volume, light and shadow, became more and more radical, much to the horror of purist photographers. His work included photomontages, collages and direct interventions on the photographic negative, which produced abstract and unpredictable results. His widely-praised *Fotoformas* series, with its various shades of grey, black and white, would go on to influence many other Brazilian photographers keen to echo the vanguard movements that had emerged twenty-five years earlier in Europe. The series is regarded as the first example of photography systematically produced in Brazil for reasons other than documentation. The belated Modernists inspired by Barros saw photography as a language that was not limited to space and time, and although the foundations of their aesthetics lay in the European vanguard movements such as Surrealism and Dadaism, their output was distinct in character: in the tradition of anthropophagy as proposed by Andrade.

Just as this creativity was beginning to flourish, Brazil entered a dark chapter in its history. Between 1964 and 1985, under the military dictatorship, work of a more experimental character virtually disappeared. During the so-called *anos de chumbo* ('years of lead'), photography reverted almost exclusively to its documentary function, both as an instrument of military propaganda and also photojournalism, which could rarely express critical views due to the censorship laws imposed on

1–2.
From the 'Fotoformas'
series, Geraldo de
Barros, (1946–51)

1.

2.

the media. The censors considered photography that did not openly promote the ideals of the government (such as the work of Geraldo de Barros) subversive. No doubt because of this, not many artists worked with photography in this period. Anna Maria Maiolino was one of the few who dared to challenge the norm and her *Fotopoemação* series clearly references the lack of freedom for artists during the dictatorship.

The end of the military regime in 1985 and the subsequent democratization process gave rise to a freer and less dogmatic production of art in general, and of photography in particular. There were three key figures in this new phase of Brazilian photography: Miguel Rio Branco, Mário Cravo Neto and Claudia Andujar. By blurring the boundaries between documentary photography and a more experimental and poetic kind of approach, they created a fertile, humanistic and original field.

By the mid-1990s, amidst a climate of expanding civil liberties, (albeit with parallel problems in politics and economics), Brazil had started to open itself up to the rest of the world. A major factor was the drop in import taxes, which were previously so high that they made access to foreign goods, including cultural items, prohibitive. New information technology also played a role, with the Internet creating virtually limitless possibilities for research, interaction and knowledge exchange. All this was to have a direct impact on the country's photographic output—particularly with regard to subject matter. If, before that period, social issues such as national identity—something that had to be slowly pieced together out of the ruins of the military regime—had been considered the most relevant topic, this new era represented a paradigm shift. Artists started to take a more subjective, erratic and ironic approach, in which the subject's interior world invariably prevailed over socio-political issues. New technologies simplified the photographic process, compelling many artists from areas as diverse as painting, cinema, performance art and sculpture to start adopting it in various stages of their creative work. They used photography in a way that was free of the dogmas, limits and censorship previously imposed on photo-documentarists, decisively contributing to the formal and conceptual expansion of photography. It was through this attitude that contemporary production reconnected with the experimentation carried out by Brazilian Modernists.

In the last decade, however, Brazil has seen deep changes re-emerge in the relationship between man and photography—a reflection of what has happened around the globe. The improvement and dissemination of digital cameras, of the Internet and its social networks, and of smartphones, for example, has raised the production rate and speed of circulation of photography exponentially. This new popularization of photography has also uncovered its duality—its ability to both record the visible world and to create parallel worlds. Reality and fiction, after all, have always been inseparable in the photographic weave. Yet, rather than destabilizing the medium, this deconstruction of the smoke and mirrors that characterize photographic production has instead expanded its potential. As demonstrated by the work produced in the first decade of this century, the debate about manipulation, truth and banality that prevailed in the 1990s led to a degree of reflection about photography that resulted in paradigmatic changes both in the documentary and in the experimental and artistic fields—in fact, making the distinction between the two even more tenuous.

New technologies, such as broadband Internet and image treatment software, have had their biggest effect on the production and circulation of images. In Brazil, it took slightly longer than in Europe and in the United States for the impact to be felt — partly due to legislation that makes it difficult to import new technology.

Nevertheless, photography today is easy, accessible and instant, and such a shift in image production has forced us to change the way we think about how we take photographs and what we take them of. Artists have also had to change the way in which they work. For Brazilian researcher Arlindo Machado, the advance of digital cameras, the Internet and mobile phone technology since the 1990s has created a fertile field for experimentation in photography not seen since the post-World War I period, when the Dada and Surrealist movements first emerged. According to Machado, 'it is not by chance that these anamorphic characteristics (manipulations and interferences on the raw material produced by the camera) are making it possible for photography to recover the demolishing and deconstructive spirit of the historical vanguard movements of the early twentieth century'.

In Brazil, this transformation was compounded in 2002 when the Ministry of Education and Culture approved the country's first university degree in Photography, taught by SENAC-SP. Previous generations of photographers, most of whom were self-taught, could rarely find professors prepared to foster reflection and supervise works focused on technical or experimental images. Since then, many other undergraduate and graduate courses have opened in universities around the country and the huge abyss between production and critical reflection has gradually begun to reduce.

The rise in popularity of university-taught photography courses has also meant that publishers have started translating more works on photography theory, and Brazilian academic output is gaining visibility, albeit slowly, in book shops. Finally, the availability of doctoral theses and Master's dissertations on the Internet has helped make access to such texts more democratic and expand the repertoire of those who combine production and research.

However, the popularization of digital photography and of image treatment software has created a perception among the general public that all images are ideological and subjective constructs. Indeed, the sector that has suffered the most from the unveiling of the magic of post-production image software and the subsequent suspicion about the veracity of images is photojournalism. As photographers of all backgrounds and abilities have become acquainted with resources that allow one to easily alter the content and appearance of an image, the very idea of photography as undisputed evidence of truth and fact has been called into question. The Catalan artist and scholar Joan Fontcuberta defines this issue such: 'Every photograph is a piece of fiction that presents itself as true. Contrary to what we have been taught, contrary to what we are used to thinking, photography always lies, it lies instinctively, because its nature does not allow it to do otherwise. But the important issue is not this inevitable lie. The important issue is how the photographer uses it, and whom he intends to serve. The important issue, in short, is the control exerted by the photographer to impose an ethical direction to his lie. The good photographer is the one who "lies the truth well"'.

Many image professionals left the newsrooms as the market became more restricted and the space dedicated to photographic reporting succumbed to the need for print media to prioritize advertisements (as a reaction to the drastic fall in the number of subscribers, who had been migrating to online news sites). The Internet did, however, present its own advantages. It has become an efficient platform for documentary photographers to renew their professional experiences. With a camera and a computer, a photographer becomes a photo agency.

Unrestricted by the bosses and editors that filtered their photographs according to the ideologies of the journalistic vehicle, these professional photographers can now tell the stories that interest them, in the way they think is most appropriate, publish the amount of photographs that they judge necessary on their websites and, moreover, sell their work to print or online media based anywhere in the world. These possibilities, which have already become the norm, represent a huge shift when compared to the routine of photojournalists a few years ago.

The 2013 protests that saw millions of people take to the streets to show their indignation at various social injustices have sparked, amongst many other discussions, a heated debate about the mainstream media's ties with the government — a significant part of the media survives thanks to the advertisement budgets of government agencies. Out of this crisis emerged a young and idealist collective of independent reporters and photojournalists who called themselves the *Mídia Ninja* (Ninja Media). Taking a no-censorship approach, and using social networks as a platform, their videos and photographs of the protests, which were taken mainly on smartphones, aimed to convey a pluralistic point of view, in opposition to the many publications that merely branded the protesters as 'troublemakers'. This is just one more example of a new generation taking advantage of new technologies and using photography and communication networks not only as receptors, but also as generators of information.

By articulating itself within this expanded, less dogmatic territory, photography — an indisputable feature of this new Brazilian generation, but still reflecting the libertarian attitude of previous generations — tends to have more humanistic and dialectical contours. This new generation of Brazilian photographers entered this new century dislodging classifications, bringing down taboos and trespassing comfort zones between languages. Brazil can now be seen from this renewed, pluralistic point of view, and less and less through the peremptory and biased perspective with which it is usually represented in foreign media.

3–4.
From the 'Fotoformas'
series, Geraldo de
Barros, (1946–51)

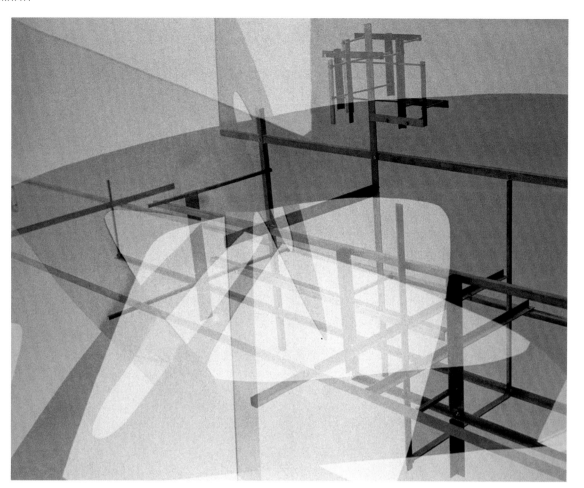

3.

4.

Cris Bierrenbach

Cris Bierrenbach was one of the most important artists in the revival of experimental photography in Brazil after the country's re-democratization. She worked as a photojournalist for the newspaper *Folha de São Paulo* from 1989 to 1992 and has since collaborated with magazines such as *Marie Claire*, *Elle* and *Vogue*.

An obsessive researcher into printing techniques, Bierrenbach is one of the few artists in Brazil who has managed to produce daguerreotypes, the earliest form of photography, and often juxtaposes nineteenth century photographic techniques with cutting edge digital technology in her work.

For the startling series *Fired* (2013) she photographed herself dressed up in the uniforms of ten different professions and then printed them at life-size before shooting a bullet through each face to mutilate and obscure it. With echoes of Chris Burden's performance art of the 1970s and the self-portraiture of Cindy Sherman, Bierrenbach's work reflects on the casual happenstance of violence at work and at home, whilst commenting on the degrading portrayal of the female body in the media and teasing the notion of everyday portraiture.

Her *Retrato Íntimo* (Intimate Portrait) series from 2003 moves in a similar direction, with x-rayed images of surgical objects and household utensils seemingly inserted into the artist's genitals in a disquieting visual play whilst *Crisbibank — Preservando Futuras Gerações* (Crisbibank — Preserving Future Generations) is a series of photographs of condoms containing the sperm of the artist's sexual partners encased in cubes of ice. Today, Bierrenbach has works in the permanent collections of the Museum of Modern Art (MAM), the São Paulo Museum of Art (MASP) and the Maison Européenne de la Photographie, Paris.

Born in São Paulo, 1964

1.

2.

3.

1.
Orange Gardens
(Labirinto), 2010

2–5.
'Fired' series, 2013

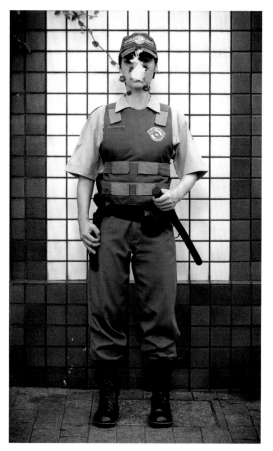

4.

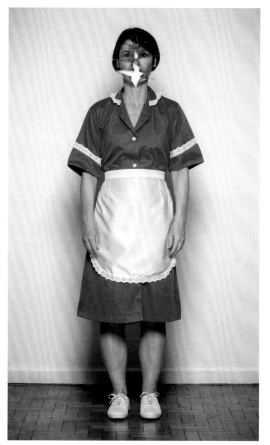

5.

Pedro Motta

Pedro Motta started his career in drawing, but became interested in photography when he realized that it allowed him to capture volumes and textures in a similar way. His images, often taken from the side of the road, document the dialogue between human and landscape, recording manmade structures as they decay or give way to nature.

In his *Archipelago* series, the road itself becomes the subject of the work, showing islands of earth where the path of construction has had to meander around telegraph poles or other fixtures on the landscape. Highlighting the on-going combat between environment and culture, his other images show manmade scars in the landscape, blood red soil contrasting with the lush greenery around them, or the facades of buildings in the city that suffered interventions after their construction. The particular way in which Motta frames his images recalls something from the aesthetics of postcards; anonymous things and places transformed into landmarks and an overarching melancholic silence.

In 2013 he was awarded the highly coveted BES Photo prize, selected due to the way in which he 'develops the perception of what is real and what is false through guesswork, suggestion and the unexpected, in his use of landscape as a traditional genre in the history of art'.

Born in Belo Horizonte, 1977

1.

2.

3.

1–2.
Arquipélago
(Archipelago) #2
series, 2008/2010

3.
Testemunho (Testimony)
#2, 2013

4.
Testemunho (Testimony)
#1, 2013

4.

Sofia Borges

Sofia Borges graduated in 2008 with a bachelor's degree in Visual Arts from the Universidade de São Paulo, and the same year received a grant for artistic research and production from the State of Pernambuco. After initially training in painting, she turned her attention to photography, taking simple, unpretentious portraits of her own family and noticing the transformation that a scene goes through to become an image: how a photo can subvert and shift meaning.

Her first photographic works were clearly influenced by cinematography, while her more recent work includes dramatically enlarged reproductions of illustrations found in science books and strong references to biology and natural history. Borges uses techniques such as digital montage, different lengths of exposure and duplication to create mysterious images that are clearly manipulated in post-production and defy classification. 'I reckon my work tries to rid photography of the so called "photographic instant"... of this idea that photography has a magical power of capturing reality and freezing a moment,' she says.

The freshness of her approach led her, at twenty-eight, to be the youngest artist to participate in the 30th São Paulo Art Biennial in 2012, although her ideas and her practice show a maturity beyond her age. Since 2013 she has held exhibitions in Mexico City, Oslo, Madrid, Paris, Lisbon, Denver, São Paulo and Rio de Janeiro with further plans for shows in London, Los Angeles, Lyon and Beijing.

Born in Ribeirão Preto, 1984

1.

1.
Rabbit, 2012

2.
80 Million Years, 2012

3.
My Sister 20 Years Ago,
2010

4.
Vampire, 2011

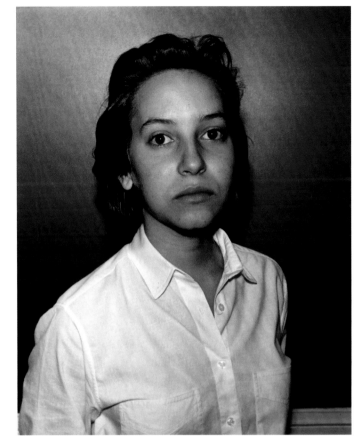

3.

2.

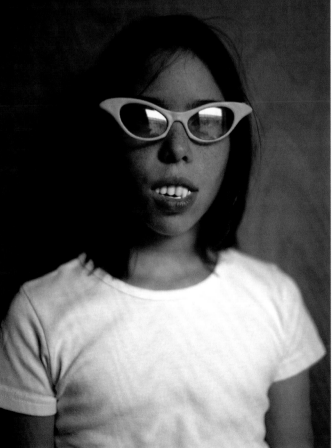

4.

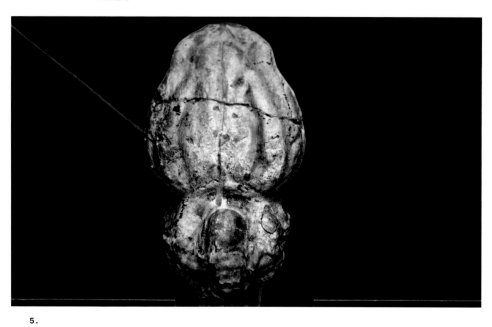

5.

5.
Artifice, 2013

6.
Still Life With a
Hammer, 2012

7.
Owl, 2012

8.
Scripts, 2013

9.
Map, 2012

10.
La Tête du Cheval, 2012

6.

7.

8.

9.

10.

Eustáquio Neves

Eustáquio Neves graduated in industrial chemistry in 1979, giving the self-taught photographer the technical skills that he would eventually take to the photography lab and apply to the manipulation of images. Since 1989 he has been researching different techniques to represent the complexity of his subject matter. Often focusing on the legacy of the slave trade in Brazil, Neves's work offers a sensitive reflection on the traditions and rituals of Brazil's black population as preserved through popular culture.

Neves layers several negatives with fragments of text before developing the images with chemical formulas in the darkroom — a process that involves a large element of chance and varying results. The blemishes, blotches and stains produced by the chemical reactions lend his work an ethereal air, as if each piece is some precious artefact, only recently uncovered and damaged by time. The content of his pictures is equally layered, often featuring haunting portraits of Brazil's Afro-Brazilian population overlaid with religious objects or decorative weapons. Neves blends different eras and cultures to reveal the juxtapositions and hidden contradictions between them.

Over the last few years, Neves has branched out from photography and experimented with short films made using low-quality equipment, embracing the background noise and flaws in representation as essential elements of the production. His work has been widely exhibited across Brazil and throughout the world with international shows in England, USA, Japan and Spain. He now lives and works in Diamantina, Minas Gerais.

Born in Juatuba, 1955

1.

2.

1.
Arturos, 1994

2–3.
Máscara de Punição
(Punishment Mask)
series, 2002–03

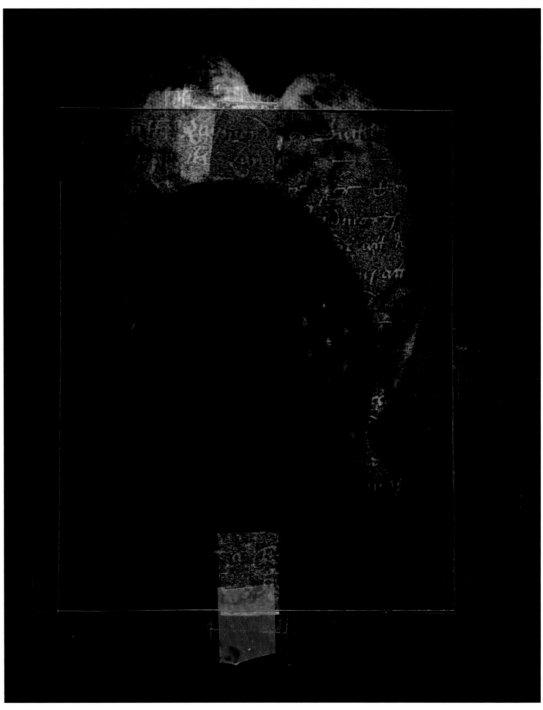

3.

very well shaped,

bout 30 years of age

long black lank Hair

long black lank Hair

4.

5.

4–6.
From the 'Oxóssi'
series, 2013

6.

Pio Figueiroa

Pio Figueiroa began his career as a photojournalist in Recife, his home city. In 2003, he founded the collective Cia de Foto along with Rafael Jacinto, João Kehl and Carol Lopes — all of whom also hail from a photojournalism background. Their work as a collective is a sophisticated reflection on the new parameters of digital photography, often in the form of innovative photo essays.

In their *Guerra* (War) series (2008) they selected pictures from their existing portfolios and treated them to recreate dramatic effects found in the work of renowned social conflict photographers such as Eugene Smith. The process resulted in a forceful set of images that emphatically conveys the atmosphere of non-declared civil war and the sensation of insecurity that prevails in many of the metropolises in developing countries.

Since November 2013, Figueiroa has turned his attention to solo projects, creating photographs and short films that still convey the same themes tackled by Cia de Foto. In the series *Marcha* (2013), he uses dramatic lighting and selective focus to highlight faces from a busy crowd in São Paulo. Shot in a powerful reportage style, Figueiroa's editing of the photos makes an innocent selection of images of commuters going about their daily routines seem like coverage of a political demonstration. In this way, Figueiroa's work deliberately blurs the line between reality and fiction, deconstructing and reconstructing the original form of an image to create a narrative.

Born in Recife, 1974

1.

2.

1.
Valparaíso, 2013

2.
Tempo Que Desmonta uma
Ação, 2013

3.
Marcha, 2013

3.

Coletivo Garapa

Founded in 2008 by photojournalists Leo Caobelli, Paulo Fehlauer and Rodrigo Marcondes, Coletivo Garapa is a photographic collective that produces content across various different platforms from the printed image to site-specific video installations. After leaving the newsroom they united efforts and founded a production company that creates both commissioned and self-initiated projects, often dealing with the challenge of telling stories from multiple sources. This research has become increasingly complex and has generated works on the border of reportage, documentary and fiction, with narrative threads constructed from collages of historical documents and testimonials shown alongside the collective's original photographs. Coletivo Garapa's works push the boundaries of direct, objective photojournalism, mixing factual and emotional, real and imaginary, past and present—some even include fictional narrators to tell their stories.

The collaborative piece *Calma* is based around a character named Rolf, a Dutchman in search of his father, who he believes is one of the unidentified casualties of the Joelma Building tragedy—a high-rise building that caught fire in 1974 killing 179 people. The project was presented in the form of a collaged mural like those found in police detective films with layers of images and ephemera connected in a web of meaning.

Inspired by the historical accounts of travellers, *A Margem* (The Riverbank) is a photographic record of the 715 mile (1,150 km) long Tietê River, the main river in the state of São Paulo and an important trade route to the interior of Brazil since colonial times. The Garapa photographers embarked on a series of expeditions, retracing the steps of the explorers who took reconnaissance missions along the river in the eighteenth and nineteenth centuries, taking photographs of the people and places they encountered and then presented them alongside historical photos, newspaper clippings and anecdotes from riverside dwellers.

Founded in São Paulo, 2008

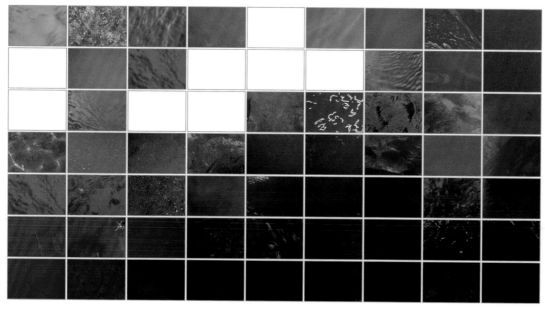

1—2.
From the 'A Margem'
series, 2013

3—4.
From the 'Calma' series
(with Thomas Kuijpers
and Lana Mesic), 2013

1.

2.

3.

4.

João Castilho

João Castilho is one of the most acclaimed Brazilian photographers to emerge over the last decade. With a degree in Literature and a Masters in Visual Arts from the Federal University of Minas Gerais, he often uses works of literature as inspiration for his photography. Such is the case with the *Whirlwind* series (2006), in which he searches for photographic metaphors to represent the manifestation of the devil in nature, according to Guimarães Rosa's 1956 novel *Grande Sertão: Veredas* (The Devil to Pay in the Backlands), one of the most important pieces of Brazilian literature.

Another important feature of Castilho's work is his particular use of colour. *Vacant Plot* is a series of photographs depicting unemployed men in an abandoned space on the outskirts of Bamako, Mali. The subjects are photographed as silhouettes in front of brightly painted walls and are deliberately anonymous: they are portrayed without identity and, therefore, without a story. More recently, Castilho has borrowed concepts from the land art tradition. His *Spice* series features various compositions of vividly coloured spices (paprika and saffron) arranged on Bolivia's stark white Uyuni Salt Flats. There is an interplay between the different materials, but also with art history: the work makes reference to painting with its activation of empty, white spaces by the introduction of red and yellow pictorial elements.

Castilho's work is present in several public collections including the MAM São Paulo and the São Paulo Museum of Art as well as the Musée d'Art Modern et d'Art Contemporain de Liège in Belgium and the Noorderlicht Gallery in the Netherlands.

Born in Belo Horizonte, 1978

1.

1.
Spice, 2009

2.
Whirlwind, 2006

3.
Land is Sky, 2007

4.
Whirlwind, 2006

2.

3.

4.

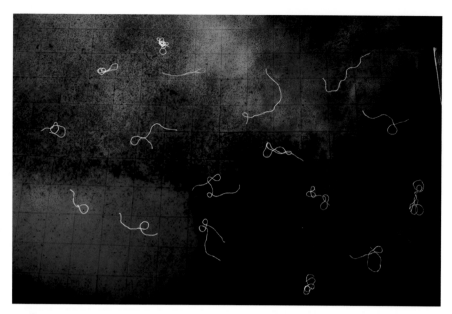

5.

6.

7.

8.

9.

10.

Barbara Wagner

Barbara Wagner graduated in Journalism and started her career working as a photographer for a number of newspapers and advertising clients in Recife. In 2005, she received a grant from the Foundation of Historical and Artistic Heritage of Pernambuco to develop a series about Brasília Teimosa, a beachside neighbourhood on the outskirts of the city. The photo essay she produced was the result of almost two years spent photographing the residents of the local *favelas* who gather at the beach every Sunday to socialize, eat, drink and swim.

'I went to Brasilia Teimosa with the idea of bringing to light issues rarely touched on directly by the media, which by nature stigmatizes issues of taste, consumerism and behaviour experienced in Brazilian lower-class neighbourhoods. During the process, what attracted me most was perceiving a particular wisdom lying behind all that energy and vulgarity that is anything but self-pitying', she said of the project.

Wagner's work explores the issues of periphery, self-representation and exoticism in the context of cultural globalization. Her portraits often draw on traditional uses of light and composition such as the chiaroscuro of Renaissance paintings juxtaposed with the desire and glamour of twentieth century editorial photography. Wagner has exhibited her photography internationally with shows at the Institute of Contemporary Arts (ICA) in London and the gallery Extraspazio in Rome amongst others. She has also completed residencies at Vitamin Creative Space in China and the Museum Het Domein in the Netherlands.

Born in Brasília, 1980

1.

1–3.
Brasília Teimosa,
2005–07

2.

3.

Rodrigo Braga

Born in the jungle-locked city of Manaus in Brazil's Amazon region, the son of two biologists, Rodrigo Braga grew up surrounded by an array of fauna and flora. It therefore comes as no surprise that much of his work deals with his relationship with nature. Although often referred to as a performance artist, the majority of Braga's work today is photographic and he has become well known for his striking images demonstrating the conflict between man and landscape, human and animal.

Braga recalls finding a sick dog as a teenager in Recife — a disturbing encounter that haunted him for years and would become the inspiration for his first work as an artist: in 2004 he acquired the body of a dead dog from an animal shelter, made a silicone cast of its face and had a veterinary surgeon sew the ears, eyes and muzzle on to a replica of his own face for a series of hyper-realist photographs titled *Compensation Fantasy*.

Braga's more recent work has a more introspective quality, featuring the artist in a state of communion with nature, naked and buried in the earth or covered in leaves and flowers. 'What enchants me about photography is the chance to disrupt time and space,' Braga says. 'I end up doing very speculative images.' He has since exhibited all over Brazil and is now represented by Galeria Vermelho, one of São Paulo's leading contemporary art galleries.

Born in Manaus, 1976

1.

2.

3.

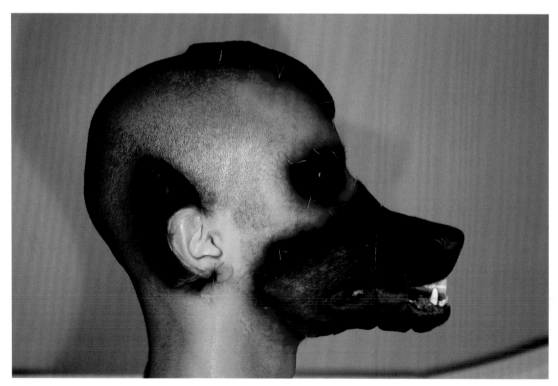

1.
Campo de Espera, 2011

2.
Desejo Eremita, 2009

3.
Comunhão I, 2006

4.
Fantasia de
Compensação, 2004

5.
Do prazer solene I,
2005

6.
Arbusto Azul, 2013

4.

5.

6.

Odires Mlászho

Odires Mlászho is a multimedia visual artist from the state of Paraná, perhaps best known for his work with photomontage. Born José Odires Micowski, even his artistic pseudonym is a kind of montage, blending the names of two of his biggest influences: Max Ernst and László Moholy-Nagy, whose works and thoughts had a great impact on his own.

Mlászho never takes his own photographs, but instead uses existing images to perform a series of 'surgeries' that aim to shift and displace their original meaning. Almost like an archaeologist seeking to give new significance to images forgotten in books and magazines, he breathes new life into old material through his particular style of collage: 'I work with images that are lost, they have been disconnected for unknown reasons... My interest is to put in this work that was abandoned, forgotten, an energy that is able to make them circulate again, but now with a new appeal, a new language. I grant their comeback in a new trajectory. I throw them back in society in the form of art'.

For his *Butchers* series Mlászho pasted together parts of the male body cut from the pages of porn magazines to compose new, surreal forms that are somehow familiar, yet at the same time completely alien: a deconstruction and re-composition of human flesh reminiscent of Frankenstein's monster. For *Cavo um Fóssil Repleto de Anzóis* (1996), he took images from an old book of black and white photographs of Roman busts and superimposed the eyes of German politicians from the 1960s. The two layers lock together almost seamlessly, giving the blank, lifeless eyes of the stone sculptures an injection of life.

Born in Mandirituba, 1960

62. EMPRESS PLOTINA. ABOUT 120 A.D. ROME, PALAZZO CAPITOLINO

1.

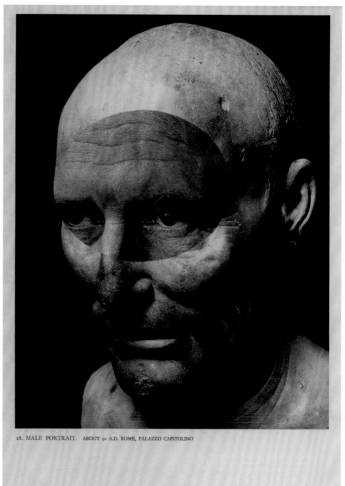

28. MALE PORTRAIT. ABOUT 30 A.D. ROME, PALAZZO CAPITOLINO

2.

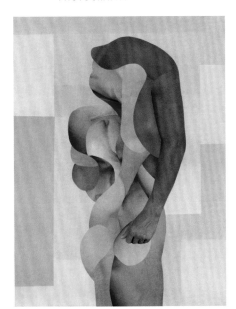

3.

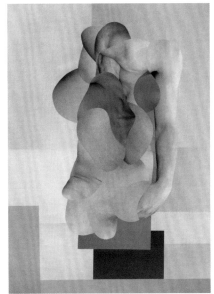

4.

5.

1.
Plotina, 1996

2.
Male Portrait, 1996

3.
Butcher IV, 2007

4.
Skinner I, 2008

5.
Butcher I, 2004

6.
Hercules Possesso I,
2010

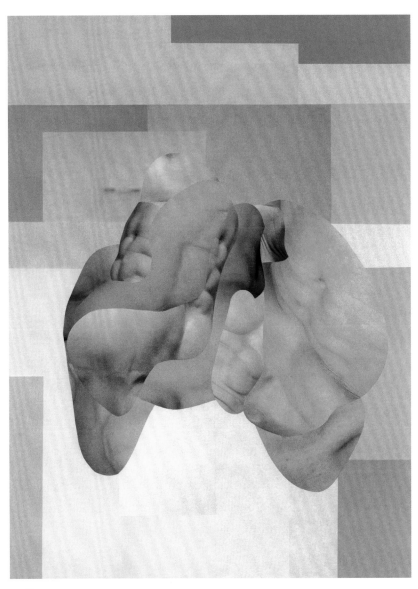

6.

279

Alexandre Orion

Ananda Nahu

Derlon Almeida

Filipe Bezerra

Fleshbeck Crew

Grupo Poro

Stephan Doitschinoff

Rimon Guimarães

Marcelo Rezende

street art

Brazilian anthropologist Gilberto Freyre is one of the principal names on the list of intellectuals who reflected upon, understood and helped build a—still diffuse—Brazilian national identity. Born to a wealthy family in the state of Pernambuco, in northeast Brazil, Freyre was a conservative and an elitist dandy, who wrote a great deal about the construction of a certain Brazilian sensuality, which he detected in the country's national history and in racial relations present during its formative years. In the 1970s, he became interested in the possibility of a new field of research: Tropicology.

Tropicology, in a definition offered by Freyre himself, intends to be a science specializing in the study of tropical things, tropical habits, peoples and cultures. It includes an ecological criterion that takes into account the land, the soil, the vegetation, the animals, the means of economical use of the soil and the subterrain of tropical spaces in many parts of the world, and studies it—anthropologically and sociologically—from the point of view of possibilities of resource management according to modern civilization criteria and of tropical values for modern civilizations. Today, more than four decades later, interpreting a culture from the point of view of its tropical experience is still used as a discourse across all kinds of artistic projects—including street art. The tropical is seen as a condition, as a spectre, as modernity and as imagination. The tropical haunts the streets.

Indeed, the tropical is certainly present in the streets of São Paulo, perhaps the logical place to start when discussing the history of Brazilian art in the public sphere. Here, in the richest, most populous and politically weighty of all the Brazilian cities, examples of street art—or urban interventions as they are sometimes known—are more common than trees, competing in number only with automobiles. There are more than 11 million inhabitants spread across a vast territory, coursing through the extensive and sometimes unbelievable grid of concrete, stone, asphalt and steel. For a while now, the city has been cultivating a network of artists, galleries and collectors (along with increased media exposure) for graffiti and *pixo (or pixação)*, a particular form of street art that consists of tagging public spaces such as walls and the facades of tall buildings with one's name or crew's name. The name comes from the Portuguese word for tar, as the first *pixadores* used the substance to daub their tags on walls and buildings as a response to government slogans and advertising. Today, most use latex or spray paint.

The origins of *pixo* lie in the historical tension between the inhabitants of São Paulo's outskirts and those of its more affluent central areas, starting with the clandestine slogans against the military dictatorship in the 1960s. Since then, it has been used by punk and hip-hop cultures and has provoked direct confrontation with established powers such as the police. This dynamic calligraphy is seen as an attack on property, and although the practice has been somewhat legitimized, especially by a small group of people in the European artistic circuit, it remains unstable and ultimately misunderstood. When a group of São Paulo *pixadores* (taggers) was invited to participate in the 7th Berlin Biennale, they ended up tagging the curator himself, because, according to them, he demanded that they offer a workshop. They claimed that *pixo* is uncontrollable, an affront, and one does not offer workshops on such things.

With graffiti, the situation has been very different. It has established friendlier relations with state forces and the other sectors of society towards which the *pixo* gangs point their spray cans. Following the pioneering work of the Choque Cultural gallery, a contemporary art gallery in São Paulo that has strong links with underground culture, graffiti artists have had their

1–2.
Street art at Beco do
Batman in the Vila
Madalena area of São
Paulo, 2014

1.

2.

works commercialized in national and international art fairs, as well as having a presence and showing vitality in the world art circuit and market. Stephan Doitschinoff (who goes by the street alias Calma) is one of the protagonists of this scene, having navigated his journey from the streets to the galleries on a wave of hysterically baroque, allegorical imagery; but the most noteworthy case is arguably that of Os Gêmeos, who have gone from the alleyways of Cambuci—a working class Italian neighbourhood in São Paulo—to meeting with Banksy in front of the international press and showing work at Tate Modern in London. Today, São Paulo's city hall even distributes a 'graffiti tour guide', including works by Os Gêmeos as well as other artists such as Nunca, Zezão and Kobra.

Street art in São Paulo is fuelled by poverty and yet celebrated on a world stage. However, to look at it simply in these somewhat conflicting terms is to forget that it is Brazilian, and that it is tropical. To consider street art in the context of Freyre's Tropicology we must explore the other regional centres of street art—a journey which takes us to the northeast, to the states of Pernambuco and Bahia, and more specifically, the city of Salvador.

Salvador is where Brazilian history began, in the early sixteenth century. The first capital of Brazil, it was often referred to as the Roma Negra (Black Rome), due to its old buildings and the strong presence of African culture, stemming from its past as a centre of slavery. A casual stroll through the city is a journey through layers of time, visible in the varying behaviours, habits and architecture.

Filipe Bezerra is a little over thirty. He lives in the Barra neighbourhood of Salvador, a district that used to be fashionable, but has been slowly decaying since the end of the last century, following the rhythm of the city as a whole. Bezerra graduated in advertising and immediately after college opened an advertising agency with some partners and started working with local clients. However, he soon started to have doubts about his metier. He left the profession and decided to become a kind of street activist, inverting the internal logic of advertising: if in advertising his goal was to create an illusion of truth about all that he touched, Bezerra decided to use advertising's language and reasoning to sell a personal truth about urban development in Salvador, its political atmosphere, the oppressive presence of media images and discourses and, of course, about the sensorial experience of life under tropical conditions.

Acorde/Discorde (Wake up/Disagree) and *Salvador Ficou Como Gregório Deixou* (Salvador Stayed the Way Gregório Left It) are two examples of the way Bezerra works. He acts in a subtle and secretive way, spreading his messages through the streets. In *Acorde/Discorde* he uses mystical, eastern iconography to create a kind of mantra. The associations that this piece evokes include the idea of a nirvana that can only be attained when there is a rupture in the relationship between Brazilians and the media. Another tactic Bezerra employs is the use of slogans and catchy taglines that he twists or perverts to subtly change their meaning. *Salvador Ficou Como Gregório Deixou* has many connotations: Gregório is a reference to Gregório de Matos, the seventeenth-century poet from Bahia whose work was characterized by political sarcasm, eschatology and a ferocious criticism of the habits of Bahia's baroque period. Bezerra focuses on the permanent sensation of vitality and degradation that has remained unchanged for centuries and comments on history repeating itself: the act of going round in circles is strikingly rendered in another of his posters that bears the slogan: *Quando Dinheiro é o Objetivo, Viver é o Obstáculo* (When Money is the Objective, Living is the Obstacle) which depicts a mouse in a wheel.

Bezerra develops his projects in a context that is very different from the one that is talked about and internationally projected by São Paulo. In Bahia, and northeastern Brazil generally, there is no market system and there are no art critics—when there is some form of legitimacy, it usually takes the form of a stamp of recognition given by institutions or events from other parts of the country. This makes the daily life of artists in the region all the more arduous, but equally, all the more free. Their existence is precarious, and the street emerges as one of the possible spaces for exhibiting works and articulating all the cultural and social forces at play.

'Nordeste' (Northeast), published in 1937, is the essay in which Gilberto Freyre first talks about the possibility of a Tropicology, and argues that the northeast is the essence of Brazil. But this is not limited to an understanding of the world through regionalism. His northeast is, by definition, cosmopolitan and culturally universalistic. What he sees as the northeastern specificity is its capacity to combine the most diverse traditions without the wish to produce a stable, finished, definitive synthesis. From this perspective, perhaps the northeast is not as 'anthropophagic' as the rest of Brazil (according to Oswalde de Andrade's theory), but something less rigid and linear.

If, then, we acknowledge that the northeast is an unstable synthesis, in Ananda Nahu's work this instability is visible. Her work is strongly charged with characters and symbols from the twentieth century, such as Jimi Hendrix and Billie Holiday. Also from Bahia, (she was born in Juazeiro, a city straddling the border of the states of Bahia and Pernambuco), Nahu has developed projects in many Brazilian cities, working under themes of a tropical, psychedelic nature and with a certain nostalgia for *tropicalismo*—the Brazilian cultural movement from the 1960s that combined art, music, literature and the desire to abolish cultural hierarchies inherited from European colonialism. Both Nahu and Bezerra end up touching upon this sensitive subject. The motive behind the *tropicalismo* movement was to eradicate the good taste of an urban middle-class that did not recognize itself as Brazilian, and longed for a clearer, cleaner and tidier image in the mirror—thus, Nahu's Jimi Hendrix somehow makes sense standing side by side with the orishas of candomblé (spirits from the Afro-Brazilian religion) and Bezerra's Eastern iconography takes on new meaning.

Home to Derlon Almeida, Recife is the captial city of Pernambuco State. With a degree of anxiety to fulfil an ideal of cosmopolitanism, Recife's cultural movements have essentially oscillated between different forms of nationalism and regionalism. It is an exemplary case for Tropicology, and under these circumstances, Almeida has opted for a rather ambitious path: to work with a repertoire of images from the state's xylographic (wood-block printing) tradition. Much of his inspiration comes from *cordel* literature, which has circulated in the northeastern region since the sixteenth century and was one of the first ways of desseminating written texts. Literally meaning 'string' literature, they are usually presented as popular and inexpensive pamphlets, often containing folk novels, poems and songs, and making intense and expressive use of xylography—converting it into a typical language form and creating visual codes and representations that have been maintained for generations. Derlon does not intend to modernize or deconstruct this inheritance, but to duplicate it. His concern is how to produce graffiti and act upon urban (and rural) spaces in a way that establishes true contact with this form of communication.

As a result, his graffiti (and his collages and stencils) are reminiscent of the xylograph technique imitated on walls, doors and many other surfaces. Derlon has also been producing work in formats that are suitable for galleries and collectors, seeking to bring his work closer to paintings. But his real force lies in this detachment, in which xylography is detached from its own limitations and the *cordel* imagery invades public spaces, presenting itself in another way, over urban surfaces and before its inhabitants.

The last decade or so, since the turn of the century, has been one of frenzy (and not necessarily in a good sense) for Brazil and for Brazilians. The country, which formerly lived in the drama of its isolation, whilst at the same time feeling comfortable within it, has been moving forwards, in search of a new, less protected experience. In this context, it appears that there is no easy path to be followed. Grupo Poro, constituted of Brigida Campbell and Marcelo Terça-Nada, warns that the challenge brought by this present is the larger problem. For more than ten years, they have been working to build new relationships between cities and their citizens, or between humankind and the landscape, through what they classify as the 'art of connection'. In one of their manifestos, they demand, 'We want parks and gardens everywhere. Less cars, more trees. More love, less engines! The city must offer pleasure'.

As part of this campaign, Poro has established the project *Political Advertising is Lucrative*, distributing pamphlets announcing a 'Professional Course on Shamelessness', hanging banners on the streets saying 'Waste Time', 'Bury Your TV' or 'Break Through Appearances', and even gluing on/off switches to lampposts. They aim to create a kind of parentheses around our daily experiences and capture the real by means of ephemeral actions: their strategies have helped them avoid what may be the most constant danger among street art movements: simply decorating the real, rather than capturing it.

The urban development of the cities in which these artists work—the backdrop against which all this work is developed—has, in the past two decades, accelerated rapidly, exerting an enormous impact on the social life of these capital cities. The trend for a lifestyle that abandons the streets in favour of workspaces or spaces for consumption has imposed new rules of surveillance, and this has translated into an intense domestication of activities performed on the streets, at least in respect to their original political potential. What the future will make of this remains a mystery: will this production represent merely a charming and unforgettable moment of Brazil's relationship with the world, and only that (think of bossa nova), or will it be able to maintain a dialogue with history, finding different modes of operation in order to promote a real return to the political?

3.
Os Gêmeos mural on the corner of Houston and Bowery, New York, USA, 2009

4.
Museu Aberto de Arte Urbana, Zona Norte, São Paulo, 2014

3.

4.

Alexandre Orion

Alexandre Orion, an arts graduate from São Paulo, completed his first graffiti project in 1992 at the age of fourteen. 'There is so much graffiti out there,' he says, 'people walk by and don't even notice it. I am trying to show people how to interact with it'.

His *Metabiótica* (Metabiotics) project does just that. Through photography and an aerosol can, Orion addresses the issues of Brazilian urban culture with his humorous and thought-provoking scenarios. These stenciled graffiti designs, inspired by the characteristic black tar of traditional *pixação* become interactive urban interventions, allowing unsuspecting passers-by to engage in brief moments of joy and anguish, surprise and suffering.

Reality meets fantasy in Orion's photographic record of the series, which plays on the humour of these interactions. It is unclear whether these perfect encounters are a question of fortuitous timing or staged by the artist—real life and art combine to create a new reality, challenging the idea that all that is photographed is real.

In 2006, Orion created *Ossário*, an intervention in one of São Paulo's busiest underpasses, using pieces of cloth to create the outlines of a multitude of skulls in the thick layer of soot that coats the walls. Thus, the tunnel became a catacomb of over 3,500 skulls—a haunting reminder of the damaging impact of fumes and pollution on the environment and our health. The work was completed at night and was hampered by numerous police checks, deafening traffic and even a team of municipal workers turning up to remove the remaining grime.

Born in São Paulo, 1978

1.

2.

1–2.
Metabiótica, 2006

3.
Sierra Sam, 2011

4–5.
Metabiótica, 2006

3.

4.

5.

Ananda Nahu

Originally hailing from Juazeiro on the border between Bahia and Pernambuco states, Ananda's vibrant pieces are carefully crafted designs that reflect the colours and rhythm of life in northeast Brazil. Nahu moved to Salvador to study graphic design and visual arts, and her research into placard and poster design history, coupled with her experiments in lithography, engraving and screen printing, inspired her to make a practical application of her studies on the streets of Salvador.

She started out with simple posters pasted on to empty walls, but soon turned her attention to the wall itself. As she became familiar with the language of street painting she began to paint ever more elaborate murals and developed her distinctive stencil technique. Nahu's work is entirely handcrafted, from cutting the stencils out of layers of transparent acetate, to the application of the colour itself, using multiple techniques and materials including charcoal, pastel, pencils, sewn canvas, paint and acrylic ink.

Her inspiration comes from a wide range of sources, including psychedelic album cover art and traditional fabrics: 'My paintings are the result of the mixture of my influences… everything from album covers, posters and banners to religious manifestations in painting and African and Asian textiles,' she explains. Her vibrant murals often look like huge swathes of brightly patterned cloth wrapped around the walls and buildings of the city.

Born in Juazeiro, 1985

1.

1–3.
Murals in Recreio
neighborhood, Rio
de Janeiro, 2013–14

2.

3.

Derlon Almeida

Derlon Almeida's earliest memory is of drawing. As a teenager he would stare at the street art on the walls of his native Recife from the window of the school bus, dreaming of creating his own. Today he is one of the most important names in Brazilian street art and his creations can be found on walls and buildings around the world.

His distinctive style is heavily inspired by the xylographic (wood-block printing) tradition, a technique used in *cordel* literature—a type of local story-telling comic book that has been popular in the northeast region of the country since the sixteenth century. Almeida does not intend to modernize or deconstruct this inheritance, but to duplicate it, mixing in a unique blend of Brazilian popular culture, iconography and pop art. He also says he is influenced by the work of late Brazilian painter, printmaker and designer Gilvan Samico.

As well as street art, Almeida creates illustrations for magazines, publicity agencies and the fashion industry, and more recently has designed pieces for a number of different institutions. He has his own studio, and takes on commissions, but still finds time at the weekends to get on his bike with his paints and find a blank wall. He has showcased his work in London, Amsterdam and Lisbon, and has had several exhibitions throughout Brazil.

Born in Recife, 1985

1.
Mural in Garanhus

2.
Mural in Triunfo

3–4.
Murals in Recife

1.

2.

3.

4.

5.

6.

7.

5.
Mural in Recife

6.
Mural in Crato

7.
Mural in Olina

8.
Mural in Lisbon,
Portugal

9.
Mural in Newcastle, UK

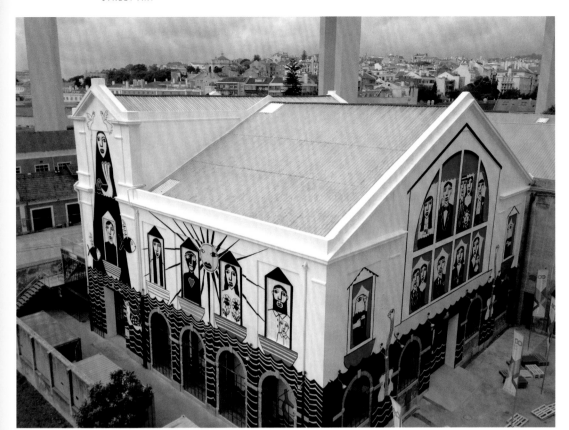

8.

9.

Filipe Bezerra

Filipe Bezerra lives and works in the Barra neighbourhood of Salvador, where he creates his distinctive brand of street art. Bezerra graduated in advertising, and for a while ran his own advertising studio, but left the profession to become a kind of street activist — his works often include slogans or taglines which encourage people to challenge the way they think, or live their lives.

Acorde/Discorde (Wake up/Disagree) incorporates eastern iconography to create a kind of mantra, evoking the idea that nirvana can only be attained when there is a rupture in the relationship between Brazilians and the media. Bezerra printed the vivid message on posters and then pasted them on walls across the city.

Often working in a colour palette of blues and yellows, Bezerra also paints commissioned pieces directly onto the walls of private houses, including the piece he titled *Plug* (2013) which depicts a domestic animal with a television for a head — a commentary on the role of TV in isolated communities.

Born in Salvador, 197

1.

1.
Acorde/Discorde, 2013

2.
Plug, Casa da Dona,
2013

3.
Calma & Sabedoria, 2013

2.

3.

Fleshbeck Crew

Fleshbeck Crew—composed of artists Bruno (BR), Bogossian, Tomaz Viana (Toz), Marcio SWK, Rod Abranches, Rogério Krrank, Leonardo Uzai (Nhôzi) and Márcio Ribeiro (Piá)—pioneered the graffiti movement in Rio, and continues to produce some of the city's most exciting work. They started out by founding the *Fleshbeck* zine, influenced by images coming out of the USA, and formulated their collective style in their sketchbooks before transforming the streets.

Their influences include graphic design and animations, 1980s Brazilian comic magazines and international graffiti artists such as Tats Cru from New York and 123 Klan from France. They mix classic American graffiti with more contemporary three-dimensional, free-form styles, and are especially known for their floating figures with long flowing hair.

Their ability to remain consistent over a period that has seen graffiti change from perceived vandalism to a respected art form is testament to the shared vision of the founding members. 'Graffiti became hip, everyone was doing it,' explains BR. 'But in the 1990s there was nothing [...] just *pixação*. Our work introduced the city to this type of graffiti and we are still obsessed with the potential. That's why we are still around, this isn't a fad for us, it's our passion.'

The Crew still work together as a team, but have also found success in their solo projects. Many of the founding members have had exhibitions in Gallery Motion in Rio de Janeiro and have participated in some of Brazil's key art events, including the São Paulo Biennial in 2010.

Founded in Rio de Janeiro, 2006

1.

1–3.
Fleshbeck Crew murals
in Rio de Janeiro,
2010–13

2.

3.

Grupo Poro

Consisting of artists Brígida Campbell and Marcelo Terça-Nada, Grupo Poro's main objective is to re-appropriate everyday urban spaces using a variety of different media. Their interventions in the abandoned construction sites, gutters, walls and streets of the city, are intended to be free from any pre-established relationships between art and the ordinary citizen. According to the artists, this means that members of the public can relate directly to these pieces, which take over the streets without having to rely on any institutions — private or public — in order to exist.

The initiative was originally conceived in 2002 by Campbell and Terça-Nada with five fellow UFMG (Federal University of Minas Gerais) students who called themselves simply O Grupo (The Group). Their first intervention involved pasting fluorescent arrows pointing at small weed stems shooting from cracks in the plaster and asphalt of the walls and pavements of Belo Horizonte, Salvador and São Paulo. The other members all went their separate ways, but Campbell and Terça-Nada carried on with what they describe as a series of 'urban interventions and ephemeral actions'. They argue that the impermanence of their work — which can last as little as just fifteen minutes — is precisely its strength.

The group's portfolio includes plastic flowers planted in neglected areas around the city, colourful vinyl letters pouring from walls and drainpipes, a project called *Azulejos de Papel* (Paper Tiles) which saw elaborate patterned paper tiles pasted on to dilapidated buildings and a series of posters carrying slogans such as *Perca Tempo* (Waste Time). In an attempt to make their work more interactive PDFs of their posters and designs are available for download on their website for people to print out at home and use themselves.

Founded in Belo Horizonte, 2002

1.

2.

3.

4.

5.

6.

7.

8.

9.

10.

Stephan Doitschinoff

Stephan Doitschinoff (also known as Calma, meaning 'calm' in Portuguese and a shortened version of *con alma*, Latin for 'with soul') is a self-taught artist, born in São Paulo, where he is currently based. The son of an Evangelical minister, Doitschinoff spent his childhood absorbing the visual vocabulary of religious art. As an artist, he has developed his own unique language and style through imagery that creatively combines Afro-Brazilian folklore with Baroque religious iconography, filling his delicate paintings with alchemic and pagan symbolism, Latin text, and elements of *pixação*.

The artist was the subject of the 2008 documentary film *Temporal*, which documented his three-year journey through rural Bahia, painting murals on the adobe houses, chapels and cemetery graves of the community, collaborating with local craftsmen in small villages throughout the region.

Doitschinoff uses various different materials to create his work: 'I use acrylics when I'm painting canvasses but when it comes to painting murals I use anything, mainly cheap house paint but also any latex, gesso, acrylics, spray, whatever I have... the only paint they used to sell at the local shop was so bad and watery that you would need two coats of black to cover other colours. Sometimes you have to improvize. I have used big chunks of charcoal to sketch the murals.'

He has exhibited in galleries in the USA, Brazil and Europe, including the Museu de Arte de São Paulo (MASP) and the Museum of Contemporary Arts of San Diego (MACSD). His work is included in The Isabel and Agustin Coppel Collection in Mexico.

Born in São Paulo, 1977

1.
A Estrela, 2011

2.
Coração Retíssimo, 2011

3.
Wooden cross in
Lençóis, 2006

1.

2.

3.

4.

5.

6.

4–7.
Murals on the walls of
Lençóis, 2006-08

7.

Rimon Guimarães

Rimon Guimarães is a young and talented self-taught artist from Curitiba. His work, which includes both street and contemporary art, as well as performance, video art, music and painting, often depicts hybrid forms and bold characters in his disntictive, colourful style. Guimarães aims to 'take people away from their monotonous daily routines and provoke them to see the street as a place where they can exchange real-life experiences,' adapting his art to the cities where he exhibits.

Originally influenced by comic books, Manga and graffiti, he now also seeks his inspiration from primitive art, Mayan culture and botanical illustrators such as Ferdinand Bauer and Ernst Haeckel. His works can be seen on streets and structures around the world, from Malaysia to the Netherlands, and has been presented in a number of international exhibitions.

Guimarães is a member of the Interlux Art Livre collective, a group of artists, musicians, philosophers and activists based in Curitiba who promote the interaction of city residents with urban spaces. He also works for Banzai Studio, a multidisciplinary creative studio, mixing commercial and personal projects on motion design, illustration, film and graffiti, collaborating with clients such as MTV, Listen Skateboards, Pernod Ricard and Nike.

Born in Curitiba, 1988

1.

2.

3.

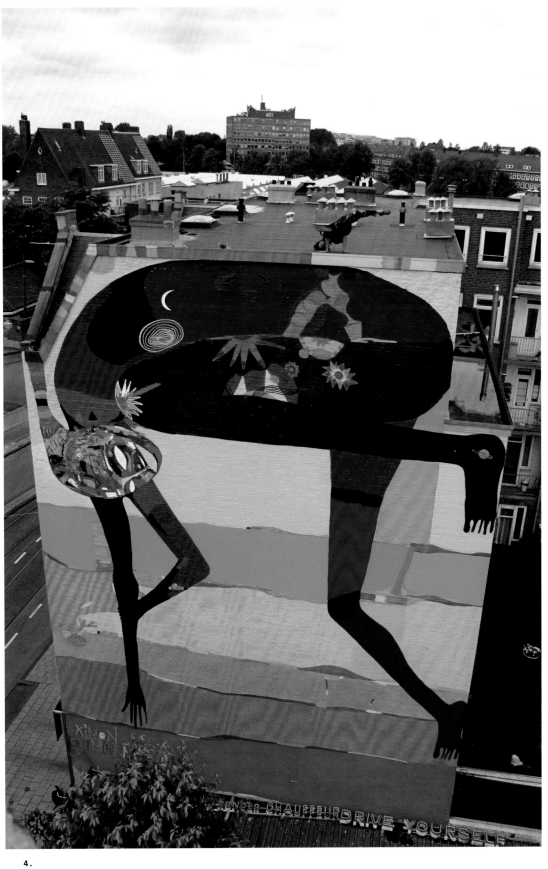

4.

5.

6.

7.

Author biographies

Alcino Leite Neto

Alcino Leite Neto is a Brazilian journalist, critic, editor and publisher of Três Estrelas, an imprint of Empresa Folha da Manhã. He writes about film and literature for the Brazilian newspaper *Folha de S.Paulo*, where he worked as cultural editor and news correspondent in Paris. He has published several articles and essays in Brazilian books and magazines, and is co-author of the books *Em Branco e Preto* (Publifolha, 2004) and *Memórias do Presente* (Publifolha, 2003). He lives in São Paulo.

Kiki Mazzucchelli

Kiki Mazzucchelli is a curator and writer working between London and São Paulo and she holds an MA in Visual Cultures from Goldsmiths College. Her recent curatorial work includes projects for the São Paulo Museum of Modern Art and SESC Piracicaba, and she has written extensively on the work of Brazilian artists. Recent publications include *The São Paulo Biennial and the Rise of Contemporary Brazilian Art* (in *Contemporary Art Brazil*, Transglobe, 2012) and the São Paulo chapter of *Art Cities of the Future* (Phaidon, 2013).

Samantha Pearson

Samantha Pearson is a prize-winning British journalist who moved to Brazil in 2010. She is currently the Brazil correspondent for the *Financial Times* and has previously worked for Reuters, *The Times*, and *The Independent*, regularly contributing on both Brazilian and international television and radio programmes. She has also worked in Mexico, Israel and East Timor. Pearson graduated in Spanish and Portuguese literature from Cambridge University and has a foundation diploma in art and design from London's Camberwell College of Arts. She lives in São Paulo.

Mara Gama

Mara Gama is a design journalist, regularly contributing to magazines such as *Vogue*, *Harper's Bazaar* and *Select*, as well as consultancy work for the *Folha de S.Paulo* newspaper. She was co-curator of the *My Waste is Your Waste* project (São Paulo, 2012 and Breda, Holland, 2013) and since 2008 has edited and produced content on design for blogs *BlogDesign* and *maragama.com*. Gama has been on the judging panel for many design awards including The House (2011), Tok & Stok (2010), Movelsul (2010) and Museu da Casa Brasileira (2008, 2007, 2006).

Ana Vaz Milheiro

Ana Vaz Milheiro is professor of Theory and History of Portuguese Architecture at the Lisbon University Institute (ISCTE) and a researcher at the DINÂMIA'CET, also in Lisbon. She holds a PhD in Architecture from the University of São Paulo and has published a number of titles including *A Construção do Brasil — Relações com a Cultura Arquitectónica Portuguesa* (2005) and *Nos Trópicos sem Le Corbusier — Arquitectura Luso-africana no Estado Novo* (2012).

Simone Esmanhotto

Simone Esmanhotto is a Brazilian journalist currently based in Paris. She is Brazil correspondent for WWD and editor-in-chief of *Veja Luxo*, a high-end lifestyle magazine. She has collaborated with *Vogue*, *Marie Claire* and *InStyle* and previously worked as fashion features editor for *Elle*.

Rodrigo Fonseca

Film critic, writer and editorial producer, Rodrigo Fonseca is drama analyst at TV Globo, Brazil's biggest TV Channel. He writes for *O Globo* newspaper and *Metrópolis*, a Portuguese magazine. Publications include *Meu Compadre Cinema — Sonhos, Saudades e Sucessos de Nelson Pereira dos Santos* (2005) and *Cinco Mais Cinco — Os Melhores Filmes em Bilheteria e Crítica* (2007). Fonseca has also worked as an actor.

Paulo Terron

Paulo Terron is a journalist who covers the Brazilian entertainment scene for both print and online publications as well as radio. He has worked for teenage magazine *Capricho*, music publication *Bizz* and edited *Rolling Stone Brasil*, as well as hosting *Qualquer Coisa*, a radio show for Oi FM. Terron wrote, produced and narrated a series of videos called *Abril em Pequim* and also created, co-wrote and co-directed a pilot episode of the sitcom *Aluga-se* for the national cable channel Multishow.

Rafael Mantesso

Rafael Mantesso graduated in marketing from São Paulo's ESPM (Escola Superior de Propaganda e Marketing) before working as Art Director for communications brand JWT, and later in marketing and branding roles for L'Oreal. Today he runs the blog *Marketing na Cozinha*, writing about current food trends, and is co-owner of the Belo Comidaria restaurant in Belo Horizonte. His creative approach to food writing caught the attention of Alex Atala, who invited him to become one of the founders of the Instituto ATÁ, created to promote Brazilian food, producers and the environment.

Eder Chiodetto

Eder Chiodetto is curator of photography at the São Paulo Museum of Modern Art (MAM-SP). He has curated more than 60 exhibitions around the world and is on the judging panel for numerous photography awards such as Paris Photo, PhotoEspaña, World Photography Organization (London) and Fotográfica Bogotá. Publications include *Curadoria em Fotografia: Da Pesquisa à Exposição* (Funarte, 2013), *Geração 00: A Nova Fotografia Brasileira* (Edições SESC, 2013) and *O Lugar do Escritor* (Cosac Naify, 2002).

Paulo Werneck

Curator of Flip (Festa Literária de Paraty), Brazil's most respected literary festival, Paulo Werneck is an editor, journalist and French translator. Werneck worked as an editor for Brazilian publishers Companhia das Letras and Cosac Naify and is co-author of a number of titles including *Cabras — Caderno de viagem* (Unisol, 1999/2002). He was also the editor of literary magazine *Ácaro*, and *Ilustrissima*, the literary and features section of the *Folha de S.Paulo* newspaper.

Marcelo Rezende

Marcelo Rezende is currently director of the Bahia Museum of Modern Art (MAM-BA). Author of the novel *Arno Schmidt* (Planeta, 2005) and of the essay 'Ciência do Sonho: A Imaginação Sem Fim do Diretor Michel Gondr' (Alameda, 2005), he has co-curated the projects *Comunismo da Forma* (São Paulo, 2007 and Toronto, 2009) and *À la Chinoise* (Hong Kong, 2007). Rezende was also the content director for the programme 'Cultura e Pensamento' (2006–11), for the Brazilian Ministry of Culture.

Index

Picture Credits

Courtesy Adriana Barra: 130, 131, 132, 133; Courtesy Adriana Degreas: 145; © Alex Robinson/JAI/Corbis: 13; Alexandre Ermel: 155bmr, 161b, 162, 163tl, 171b; Courtesy Alexandre Herchcovitch: 142, 143; Courtesy Alexandre Orion: 288, 289; Courtesy Ananda Nahu: 290, 291; Andre Nazareth: 91, 92; Courtesy Antonio Bernardo: 134; Courtesy Arnaldo Antunes: 236; Courtesy Barbara Casasola: 138, 139, 140, 141; © Barbara Wagner: 272, 273; Beto Felício, courtesy Galeria Luisa Strina: 80; Blaise Adilon/Bienal de Lyon, courtesy Galeria Vermelho: 68, 69; Courtesy Caetano Veloso: 240r; Courtesy Campana Brothers: 114, 115, 116, 117; Carlos Kopnis, courtesy GrupoSP: 39b; Courtesy Carlos Motta: 96, 97; César Charlone: 160br; Cia de Foto: 155br, 163m; Courtesy Claudia Leitte: 239; © Coletivo Garapa: 266, 267; Courtesy Criolo: 237; © Cris Bierrenbach: 252, 253; Courtesy Daniel Filho: 172, 173; Daniel Steegmann and Renata Lucas, courtesy Galeria Luisa Strina: 81tl; Courtesy Daniel Trench & Celso Longo: 212, 213, 214, 215; Daniela Nader: 158; David Prichard: 170t; Courtesy Derlon Almeida: 293, 294, 295; Ding Musa, courtesy Galeria Vermelho: 73tr; Courtesy Domingos Totora: 110, 111; Edouard Fraipont, courtesy Galeria Luisa Strina: 64, 65bl, 65br, 66, 67t, 67b, 73tl; Edu Simoes: 185r; Eduardo Eckenfels: 53b; Eduardo Ortega, courtesy Galeria Fortes Vilaça: 62, 63tl, 63bl, 63br, 83t, 83bl, 83br; Courtesy Elaine Ramos: 216, 217; © Eustáquio Neves: 260, 261, 262, 263; © Fabiana de Barros: 247, 251; © Fairchild Photo Service/Condé Nast/Corbis: 147, 149bl, 149br; Fernando Guerra, courtesy Isay Weinfeld: 42tl, 42tr, 42bl, 42br, 44b, 45b; Courtesy Fernando Meireles: 155bml, 155bl, 160t, 160bl, 161t; Courtesy Fernando Prado: 98, 99, 100, 101; Filipa Alves, Courtesy Galeria Fortes Vilaça: 76t, 76b; Courtesy Filipe Bezerra: 296, 297; Filipe Borba, courtesy Emicida: 231; Courtesy Fleshbeck Crew: 298, 299; Fotograma: 171; Courtesy Gal Costa/Guto Costa: 241l, 241r; Courtesy Galeria Luisa Strina: 81bl, 81r, 86, 87t, 87b; Courtesy Galeria Mendes Wood DM: 78l, 78r, 79t, 79b; Courtesy Galeria Vermelho: 69bl, br, 70, 71,72, 73b; Courtesy Grupo Poro: 300, 301, 302, 303; Courtesy Heitor Dhalia: 155tl; © HELVIO ROMERO/dpa/Corbis: 146r; © Ian Trower/JAI/Corbis: 60t; © Ian Trower/Robert Harding World Imagery/Corbis: 60m, 60b; Ibid Projects, courtesy Galeria Fortes Vilaça: 74, 77; Ilana Lichtenstein: 163tr, 163b; Instituto Moreira Salles: 19t, 19bl, 19br; Courtesy Jack Vartanian: 135; Courtesy Jader de Almeida: 102, 103; © João Castilho: 268, 269, 270, 271; Courtesy João Filgueiras Lima: 32, 33; Courtesy Jorge Furtado: 166; Courtesy José Padilha: 159b; © JUANJO MARTIN/epa/Corbis: 243; Rubens Kato: 177t, 177m, 177b, 179t, 179b, 185l, 283t, 283b, 287; Kerry Hayes/Columbia Pictures: 155tr, 159tr; Courtesy Kiko Farkas: 220, 221, 222; Kirsten Johnson: 170b; Courtesy Kleber Mendonça Filho: 155tml, 167tr, 167b; Courtesy Laís Bodanzky: 155tmr, 164, 165t, 165b; Courtesy Lenny Niemeyer: 125; Leonardo Finotti, courtesy Carla Juaçaba: 40, 41; Leonardo Finotti, courtesy Isay Weinfeld: 43t, 43m, 43b, 44t, 45t; © Macduff Everton/Corbis: 10; © Marcelo Fonseca/Demotix/Corbis: 149t; Courtesy Marcelo Rosenbaum: 104, 105, 106, 107; © MARCELO SAYAO/epa/Corbis: 121; Courtesy Marcio Kogan: 26, 27, 28, 29; Marcos Hermes: 240; Mariana Chama: 95; © Mauricio Santana/Corbis: 122tl, 122tr, 235, 242; Nelson Kon, courtesy MMBB: 34, 35, 36, 37; © 2014, The Museum of Modern Art/Scala, Florence: 53t; Courtesy Natalie Klein: 144; Nelson Kon: 25tl, 25tr; Nelson Kon, courtesy Brasil Arquitetura: 46, 47t, 47m, 47b; Nelson Kon, courtesy GrupoSP: 38, 39t; Nelson Kon/Andres Otero: 25b; Octavio Cardoso: 188, 189t, 189m, 189b; © Odires Mlászho: 278, 279; Courtesy Os Gêmeos: 286; Courtesy OVO: 108, 109; Paprica Fotografia 169b; Courtesy Paula Cademartori: 136, 137t, 137m, 137b; Paula Prandini: 153t; © Paulo Fridman/Corbis: 9; Paulo Melo Jr, courtesy Derlon Almeida: 292, 293br; Courtesy Paulo Mendes da Rocha: 30tl, 30bl, 30br, 31t, 31b; © PAULO WHITAKER/Reuters/Corbis: 146l; Courtesy Pedro Lourenço: 126l, 126r, 127t, 127bl, 127bml, 127bmr, 127br, 128tl, 128tr, 128bl, 128br, 129; © Pedro Motta: 254l, 254r, 255l, 255b; Pedro Motta, courtesy Galeria Luisa Strina: 65t; © Pio Figueiroa: 264, 265t, 265b; Courtesy Racionais MC's: 238tl, 238b; Courtesy Racionais MC's/Rodrigo Acedo: 238tr; © RAHEL PATRASSO/Xinhua Press/Corbis: 148t; Courtesy Rico Lins: 224l, 224r, 225t, 225b; Courtesy Rimon Guimarães: 308l, 308tr, 308br, 309, 310t, 310b, 311; Rivane Neuenschwander, courtesy Galeria Fortes Vilaça: 82, 84b; Courtesy Roberta Sudbrack: 186, 187t, 187b; © Rodrigo Braga: 274, 275, 176t, 276b, 277t, 277b; Courtesy Rodrigo Teixeira: 168, 169t, 169m; Sebastiano Pellion di Persano, courtesy Galeria Fortes Vilaça: 75; © SEBASTIAO MOREIRA/epa/Corbis: 122b; Sergei Illin, courtesy Galeria Vermelho: 71br; Sergio Coimbra: 183t, 183bl, 183br, 190, 191, 192t, 192m, 192b, 193, 194, 195t, 195m, 195b, 196, 197tl, 197tr, 197b, 198, 199t, 199b, 200tl, 200tr, 200b, 201, 202, 203tl, 203tr, 203ml, 203mr, 203b; © Sofia Borges: 256, 257t, 257bl, 257br, 258t, 258b, 259t, 259ml, 259bl, 259br; Courtesy Stephan Doitschinoff: 304l, 304r, 305, 306t, 306b, 307t, 307b; © THIAGO BERNARDES/dpa/Corbis: 148b; Thomas Strub, courtesy Galeria Fortes Vilaça: 63tr; Tim Lanterman, courtesy Galeria Fortes Vilaça: 85; © Tim Tadder/Corbis: 15; Courtesy Tunga: 57; Courtesy UNA Arquitetos, photo Nelson Kon: 48, 49t, 49m; Courtesy UNA Arquitetos, photo Bebete Viégas: 49b; Vicente de Mello, courtesy Galeria Fortes Vilaça: 84t; Victor Juca: 167tl; Courtesy Walter Salles: 153m, 153b; XX: 207; © Yadid Levy/Robert Harding World Imagery/Corbis: 11; Courtesy Yomar Augusto: 218l, 218r, 219t; Courtesy Yomar Augusto. Producer: Robert Valdes (Head Of Production); Art Director: Mike Quattrocchi; Creative Director: Sue Anderson; Art Buyer: Julia Menassa (Senior Art Producer); Copywriter: Amy Lieberthal; Photographer: Hibbard Nash; Creative Director: Hoj Jomehri; Chief Creative Officer: Mark Figliulo: 219bl, 219br; Courtesy Zanini de Zanine: 112, 113t, 113b; Zazen Produções: 159tl

Every reasonable effort has been made to acknowledge the ownership of copyright for photographs included in this volume. Any errors that may have occurred are inadvertent, and will be corrected in subsequent editions provided notification is sent in writing to the publisher.

Phaidon Press Limited
Regent's Wharf
All Saints Street
London N1 9PA

Phaidon Press Inc.
65 Bleecker Street
New York, NY 10012

www.phaidon.com

First published 2014
© 2014 Phaidon Press Limited

ISBN 978 0 7148 6749 6

A CIP catalogue record for
this book is available from
the British Library.

Commissioning Editor: Emilia Terragni
Project Editor: Joe Pickard
Production Controller: Alenka Oblak

Designed by R2 Design
Printed in China

The publisher would like to thank
Carolina Chagas for her incredible
efforts in helping to make this project
a reality — we could not have made the
book without her knowledge, passion
and hard work.

We are very grateful to the many other
people that helped provide images,
texts, and countless other contribu-
tions to the title, including Sergio
Coimbra, Rubens Kato, Carina Martins,
Paulo Terron and Maria Brant.